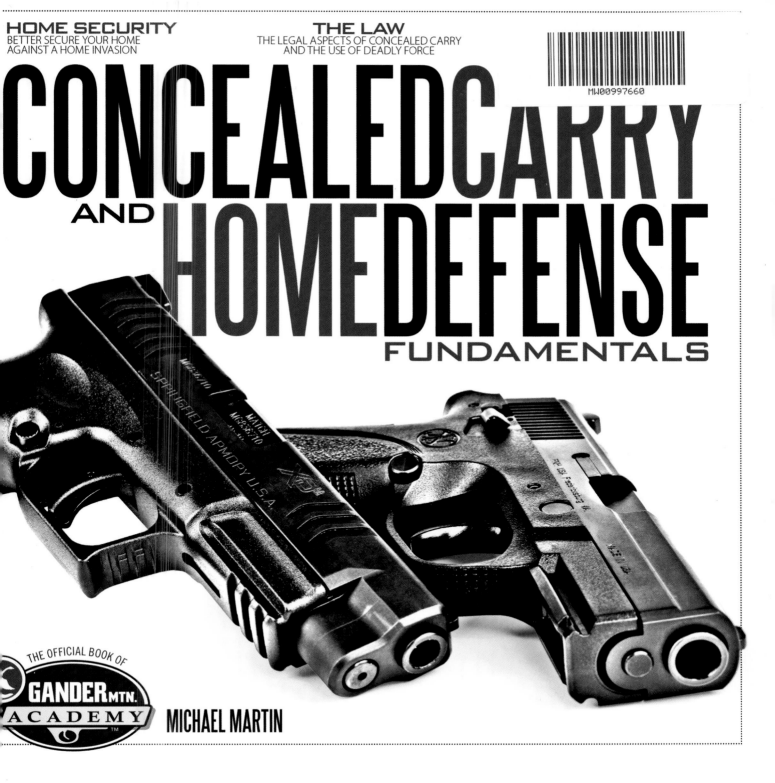

HOME SECURITY
BETTER SECURE YOUR HOME
AGAINST A HOME INVASION

THE LAW
THE LEGAL ASPECTS OF CONCEALED CARRY
AND THE USE OF DEADLY FORCE

CONCEALEDCARRY
AND HOMEDEFENSE
FUNDAMENTALS

THE OFFICIAL BOOK OF
GANDER MTN.
ACADEMY

MICHAEL MARTIN

Published by Key House Press, LLC.

Printed in the United States.

Library of Congress Control Number: 2008933390

978-1-4675-6299-7

Concealed Carry and Home Defense Fundamentals. Gander Mountain Edition.

Written by Michael Martin.

Design by Michael Martin, Ken Wangler and Dusty Reid.

Cover photo by Ken Wangler and Dusty Reid.

Cover design by Dusty Reid.

Photos on pages 1, 2, 42, 207, 209, 228, and 229 by Jon Patton, copyright© Gander Mountain Company, used by permission. Photos on pages IX, 72, 78 and 226, by Oleg Volk, used by permission. Photo on page 214 by Steve Aryan, used by permission. All other photos and illustrations are licensed for use, used by permission of the manufacturer, or are copyright© Michael Martin.

NRA and Eddie Eagle logos are trademarks of the National Rifle Association. Gander Mtn. Academy and Gander Mtn. are trademarks of Gander Mountain Company. USCCA is a registered trademark of Delta Defense, LLC. Key House Press is a registered trademark of Key House Press, LLC.

FOREWORD

Being properly educated and prepared for personal and home defense is a serious responsibility. While there are many exemplary citizens who have invested their time and resources into better preparing themselves and their families, there are far more people who are just beginning that journey. Like with any complex topic, it can be intimidating for a beginner to know just where to start. While many people may see this journey as intimidating, we see it as a great opportunity to build a proper foundation of knowledge, preparation and practice. Gander Mountain Academy is committed to the highest level of excellence in firearms training, safety, education, and innovation. As such, we are very selective when it comes to the training materials that we provide for our guests and students. This book meets that standard, and we are proud to put our name on it. The information in this book is presented in a way that best resonates with the many thousands of students we have taught in our facilities, and it includes the many theories upon which we base our classroom curriculum.

If you are an accomplished and seasoned student of personal defense, we know that you'll appreciate this book's easy to understand explanations and illustrations of topics that can confuse even experts; and if this is your very first experience with personal defense instruction, you'll walk away understanding not only the fundamentals of concealed carry and home defense, you'll also understand topics that might take years to understand otherwise. We believe this book does an extraordinary job of making expansive and complicated subjects accessible and easy to understand for even the newest beginner.

Gander Mountain Academy is proud to offer the highest quality training available. We are insistent upon delivering safe, clean, and state-of-the-art facilities with an open invitation to individuals, families, businesses, law enforcement and the military. In addition to providing live fire ranges, we are proud to offer immersive, safe, and interactive simulated ranges to more thoroughly prepare recreational, competitive, and defensive students. And now, with the release of this second edition of our book, we are more excited than ever to be able to offer this comprehensive resource to help in accomplishing our mission. This book is a must-read for anyone who takes their personal responsibility with a firearm as seriously as we do.

Be prepared...Train safe.

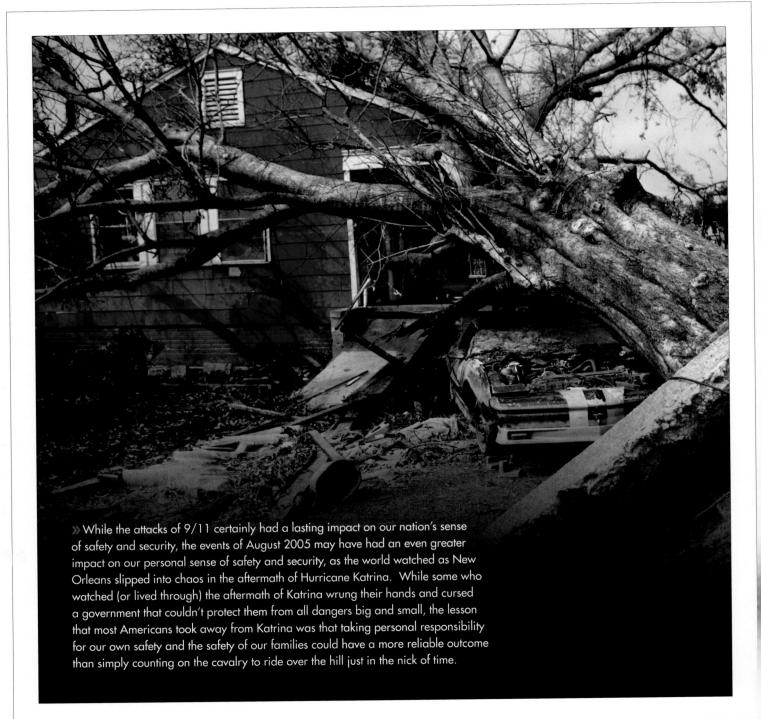

» While the attacks of 9/11 certainly had a lasting impact on our nation's sense of safety and security, the events of August 2005 may have had an even greater impact on our personal sense of safety and security, as the world watched as New Orleans slipped into chaos in the aftermath of Hurricane Katrina. While some who watched (or lived through) the aftermath of Katrina wrung their hands and cursed a government that couldn't protect them from all dangers big and small, the lesson that most Americans took away from Katrina was that taking personal responsibility for our own safety and the safety of our families could have a more reliable outcome than simply counting on the cavalry to ride over the hill just in the nick of time.

INTRODUCTION

During the last decade, there has been a seismic shift in the attitude of most Americans when it comes to the topic of firearms ownership. Generations of Americans who had been indoctrinated into believing that guns were evil were slowly giving way to a new generation that believed that not only was firearm ownership a right, but that taking personal responsibility for the safety of ourselves and our families was a responsibility. Much of this shift was due to the events of the decade. While the political assassinations of the 1960s and the rising crime rates of the 1970s and 1980s led many Americans at the time to believe that the gun was to blame, events of the 2000s and 2010s led more Americans to believe that the conclusions of the previous few decades were faulty. While the attacks of 9/11 certainly had a lasting impact on our nation's sense of safety and security, the events of August 2005 may have had an even greater impact on our *personal* sense of safety and security, as the world watched as New Orleans slipped into chaos in the aftermath of Hurricane Katrina. While some who watched (or lived through) the aftermath of Katrina wrung their hands and cursed a government that couldn't protect them from all dangers big and small, the lesson that *most* Americans took away from Katrina was that taking personal responsibility for our own safety and the safety of our families could have a more reliable outcome than simply counting on the cavalry to ride over the hill just in the nick of time.

Those changing attitudes are reflected in a recent survey by the National Shooting Sports Foundation, where people were asked about the reasons behind their most recent firearms purchase. The top two

Reasons for Last Firearm Purchase

- 40% — Home Defense
- 36% — Personal Protection
- 30% — Target Shooting
- 28% — Hunting

responses were for "home defense" and "personal protection," at 40 percent and 36 percent respectively, while "hunting" came in a distant third, at just 28 percent. A decade ago, those numbers would have been reversed. The shifting tide has also made its way into state houses across the country—for example, in the late 1980s, fewer than ten states provided law abiding citizens with the right to carry firearms for self-defense, and fewer than one million citizens were granted that right. Today, the number of "right to carry" states stands at 40 (with nine additional states offering discretionary permits), and the number of permit holders has increased to more than eight million nationwide. During that same time period, the National Rifle Association estimates that the number of legally owned firearms in the U.S. grew to more than 300 million, including an estimated 100 million handguns, yet the FBI's uniform crime report continues

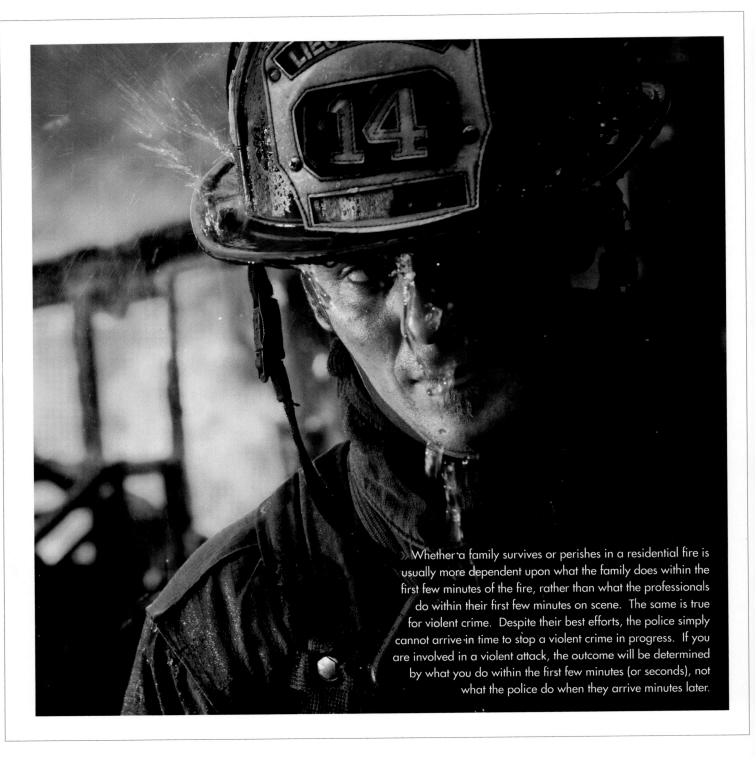

Whether a family survives or perishes in a residential fire is usually more dependent upon what the family does within the first few minutes of the fire, rather than what the professionals do within their first few minutes on scene. The same is true for violent crime. Despite their best efforts, the police simply cannot arrive in time to stop a violent crime in progress. If you are involved in a violent attack, the outcome will be determined by what you do within the first few minutes (or seconds), not what the police do when they arrive minutes later.

to show an overall *drop* in violent crime year-over-year, with a dramatic decrease in the number of deaths attributed to firearms. Collectively, those facts fly in the face of anti-gun organizations' claims that more guns equals more crime, when in fact, the opposite seems to be true, with violent crime at a 38-year low, and gun ownership (and concealed carry permits) at an all time high. So that begs the question, "Is owning a firearm right for *you*?" The decision to purchase a firearm for home defense, or a decision to apply for a permit and ultimately carry a handgun for personal protection, is a serious decision, but, it's no more serious than other decisions you've most likely made for the protection of yourself and your family, such as a decision to maintain smoke alarms and a fire extinguisher in your home, or a decision to learn CPR. Each of these decisions is nothing more than the recognition that your city's police, fire, and EMS services are not omnipresent, and will not suddenly materialize when you and your family are confronted by a fire, a heart attack, or a violent crime. When it comes to fires and heart attacks, we know that prevention matters, and the same is true

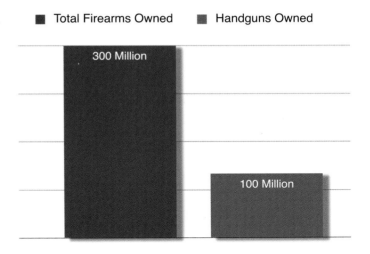

for violent crime. To that end, Chapter One will kick the book off with a variety of topics focused *entirely* on prevention, avoidance, and awareness. Within this chapter, we'll discuss how to develop a "Personal & Home Protection Plan," which helps to ensure that we're *less* likely to find ourselves in a situation where we have no other option than to use a firearm, rather than *more* likely. Chapter Two will then introduce you to a wealth of information on different types of self-defense firearms including handguns, home defense shotguns, and the AR-15 platform, and we'll provide easy to understand explanations of the common terms used so frequently. The goal of this chapter is to de-mystify what can sometimes feel like a topic reserved for experts. Chapter Three will continue with the basics, including a very visual overview of what we call the "building blocks" or the fundamentals for accurate and safe shooting. Chapter Four covers important legal topics, including the laws governing the legal use of force inside and outside the home. In this chapter, you'll get a chance to test what you've learned, using

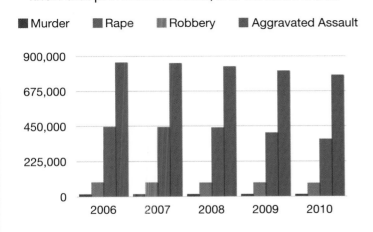

several real world scenarios. Chapter Five covers the physiology of violent attacks, including a detailed section on the automated reactions that you should expect to experience if you're ever involved in what the police refer to as a critical incident. This section will take you on an amazing tour of the inner workings of the brain, which should convince you why we take the "simple versus complex" approach in our shooting fundamentals section in Chapter Three. This chapter goes on to explain what our options might be during a critical incident, and what we should know when dealing with the police after an incident has ended. Chapter Six will introduce you to the variety of gear and gadgets available for firearm owners, including holster options and other gear such as lights, lasers, and gun vaults. Chapter Seven summarizes the book with a number of basic and advanced drills designed to take your skill level beyond the building blocks introduced in Chapter Three, and dramatically elevate your speed, accuracy, and enjoyment at the range.

Before we kick off the book, we thought we'd help answer a question that you might be asked some day: "Why do you own a firearm?" Until recently, we'd answer that question by using the analogies mentioned earlier, and we'd compare owning and carrying a firearm to taking the time to learn CPR or taking the responsibility to keep fire extinguishers in our home. We'd also have thrown out a variety of statistics to prove our point (which are included in this book), or we'd have discussed the meaning of the Second Amendment. But our answer to that question got a whole lot easier after a long day shooting photos with photographer Oleg Volk. At the end of the day, we were heading back home with Oleg trailing behind us, snapping a few last minute pictures. When we sat down to look at the results of the day, the photo on the opposite page caught our eye. Sam (then three years old) was about ready to fall asleep, and Jack (then six years old) was dragging his feet after the long day. A casual observer of this photo would tend to see nothing more than a protective father walking home with his sons, and it might take a closer look to realize that there's a firearm on the author's hip. That photo, above all others, reminded us why a firearm is included in our personal and home protection plans. Owning or carrying a firearm isn't about statistics or constitutional arguments, it's not about analogies or comparisons, it's not about the gear, and to be honest, it's not even about the gun. It's about taking a *small measure* of personal responsibility for our safety and the safety of our families. It's about making it home safe at night and being safe while in our homes. It's about recognizing that *we* are our families' first responder. And, it's about taking that responsibility seriously.

CONTENTS

>> CHAPTER 1

DEVELOPING A PERSONAL & HOME PROTECTION PLAN

Developing a personal & home protection plan is a key component of not only preparing for how we should (or might) react if confronted by a violent crime, but also how we might avoid violent crime in the first place. The first topic we'll cover in this chapter will take a look at violent crime itself in the United States, where we'll explain just how common it is compared to other risks we've already prepared for in our lives, such as the risk of injury or death due to a home fire. Within this chapter, you'll also discover that developing a protection plan is about much more than becoming proficient with a firearm or writing up a home invasion plan. It's a plan that must encompass awareness, avoidance, and preparation, so that we're *less* likely to find ourselves in a situation where we have no other option than to use our firearm, rather than *more* likely.

Think about it this way—if we only focused on becoming proficient with our firearm, but spent no time considering ways of avoiding violent crime, we'd be no different than a family who keeps fire extinguishers in strategic locations throughout their home and who runs annual fire drills, yet who fails to consider fire *prevention*, and continues with risky behavior such as leaving candles burning at night, or failing to monitor food cooking on the stove or in the oven. That family virtually guarantees that someday they'll have a chance to put their home escape plan to the test. We need to be better than that.

Topics in this chapter also include an overview of situational awareness and how we might take the idea of the President's protective bubble and apply it to our own lives. We'll expand on that topic by walking through the color codes of awareness, developed by a gentleman named Jeff Cooper, whom we've profiled in this chapter. These color codes are designed to make us more aware of our surroundings and to avoid what Cooper describes as the, "Oh my God, this can't be happening to me!" situation. The next topic will stress just how important situational awareness is, with a commentary on "Action versus Reaction."

We'll continue with a topic on "Observing Your Environment," which explains not only how to watch for and avoid areas that might be attractive to criminals, but to also look for objects in our environment that can work to our advantage. We'll also look at a number of home security ideas, and we'll have a discussion about how mental exercises can take us beyond the drills that we can run at the range. We'll wrap up the chapter with a discussion of exactly how a Concealed Carry Permit may fit into your overall plan.

How Does the Risk of Violent Crime Compare to Other Risks?

When contemplating whether or not to purchase a firearm for home defense or to obtain a concealed carry permit, many people ask the question, "Just how likely is it that I'll be a victim of violent crime?" While violent crime has been decreasing over the last three decades, it can occur anywhere, at any time. In the United States, there were more than 1.2 *million* violent crimes in 2011, including 15 thousand murders, 83 thousand rapes, 354 thousand robberies, and 751 thousand assaults. Considering the importance that most families place on smoke detectors and fire escape plans, it's worth knowing that you are more than three times as likely to be the victim of a violent crime than you are to be the victim of a residential fire, and you are more than 58 times as likely to be assaulted than you are to be injured in a home fire. Purchasing a firearm for home defense, and getting a concealed carry permit are just two small steps in developing a personal and home protection plan. Situational awareness, mental preparation, planning, conflict avoidance, and ongoing training are all components of this lifestyle to ensure that we use force as a last resort; but if required, we're prepared to defend ourselves and our families.

Violent Crime   **Residential Fires**

1.2M

300,000

Sources: FBI Uniform Crime Report; and the U.S. Fire Administration.

DEVELOPING A PERSONAL PROTECTION PLAN

What exactly is the goal of a personal protection plan? At its most basic level, a personal protection plan is designed to help keep us physically, legally, financially, and morally safe. While our personal protection plans should include becoming proficient with a firearm or other defensive tool, our ultimate goal should be to *avoid* violent encounters in the first place by developing an acute awareness of our surroundings and by making intelligent decisions about our actions, behavior, and precautions. Three options typically exist when it comes to a violent encounter: avoid the situation entirely, escape from a situation that is already in progress, or defend ourselves from a situation that we weren't able to avoid and are unable to escape from. While the choice isn't always left up to us, the topics in this chapter help to increase the likelihood that we'll have an opportunity to avoid or escape from dangerous situations *before* a use of force is required.

Conflict Avoidance

So why is avoidance or escape so important, if legally, we have the right to defend ourselves from a violent attack? The answer is more than just the fact that the only guaranteed method of surviving a violent encounter is to avoid it in the first place. It's also because the law will place a special emphasis on our decisions and actions leading up to any incident where we were in possession of a firearm, and we'll be expected to have "known better" if we could have avoided a situation that turned

violent. Prosecutors will want to know more than just, "Who was the assailant?" and, "Who was the victim?" They'll want to know *what did we do* to avoid or instigate the fight? In part, prosecutors will use what's known as the "reasonable person test." That means they'll weigh whether or not they believe a "reasonable person" would have believed the same things we believed to be true and would have reacted the same way we reacted. But here's the catch: "reasonable person" doesn't mean our friends, our family, the gang at the local shooting club, or other permit holders. It means 12 average jurors picked from the community. Because of that test, a use of force on our part must carry such seriousness attached to it that it's a fair question to ask, "Is this situation worth going to jail over?" or, "Is this situation worth dying over?" If the answer is "Yes," then we'll need to be prepared to live with the results. If the answer is "No," then we'll need to work hard to remove ourselves from the situation (quickly!) *before* the only option remaining is a use of force.

Said another way, a use of force on our part should only be done as a last resort, when we have no other choice, and when the risk of death or jail time is secondary in our minds compared to the necessity of defending ourselves from an unavoidable situation that we didn't start, and we couldn't escape from. On the next page, we've borrowed a few thoughts from one of our favorite classes, the NRA's *Personal Protection Outside the Home*, which asks some very serious questions we'll need to consider.

National Rifle Association

founded 1871

Since its founding, the NRA continues to be the leader in firearms education. Over 73,000 Certified Instructors now train about 800,000 gun owners a year. Since the establishment of the lifesaving Eddie Eagle® Gun Safety Program in 1988, more than 24 million pre-kindergarten to sixth grade children have learned that if they see a firearm in an unsupervised situation, they should "STOP. DON'T TOUCH. LEAVE THE AREA. TELL AN ADULT." With four million members and another 40 million U.S. Citizens who identify themselves as "NRA Members" (yet who fail to pay the dues), the NRA is the largest organization in the U.S. dedicated to continued support of our 2nd Amendment rights. To join, visit: www.NRA.org

Am I prepared to take the life of another human being to save my own or someone else's life? The taking of another person's life, even to save our own, would be the second worst thing that could possibly happen in our lives. The worst, of course, would be losing our own life or the life of a loved one to violent crime. But, many individuals who *did* successfully defend themselves or their loved ones from a violent attack discovered that the result wasn't euphoria at having survived. Instead, it was the guilt of knowing they took the life of another person.

Am I prepared to risk my own life or the life of a loved one? While the vast majority of violent encounters are ended when responsibly armed citizens simply expose their firearm (without firing any shots), there are no guarantees that you'll be that lucky. Think about it this way—if your behavior and actions can either put you in close proximity to a bad guy's knife, gun, or fists, or leave you hundreds or thousands of feet away, which behavior and actions are the prudent ones?

Am I prepared to tolerate the judgment of my friends, family, neighbors, and the media if I must defend myself with force? If you are involved in a shooting, however justified it may be, you should expect to be the lead story on all local TV stations and make the front page of your local papers. And that's not because you'll be getting an award. Be prepared for your attacker to be called the "victim" and for the press to use phrases like, "The prosecuting attorney has not yet decided whether charges will be filed against the shooter." Your case will be debated over water coolers and on pro- and anti-Second Amendment message boards, and you may discover that people you *thought* would be on your side are not on your side after all.

Am I prepared to go to jail over my decision? Even if a shooting is found to be justified, you should expect to spend tens of thousands of dollars defending yourself with the help of a quality lawyer who understands and has experience with self-defense cases. You should be prepared to lose your carry permit, your right to own firearms, your savings, and quite possibly your freedom.

SECONDS COUNT

After asking ourselves the difficult questions on the previous page, we'll need to remember that a use of force is not the only possible outcome when it comes to a violent encounter. The *three* possible outcomes of avoidance, escape, or defense, share a key element, and that's that seconds count. If we go through life with a complete lack of awareness of our surroundings, the first two options are typically off the table, and our ability to defend ourselves is seriously limited. Think about the warning time that each of the outcomes might require. For us to *avoid* a dangerous situation in the first place, we might need anywhere from 60 seconds to five minutes to be somewhere else. For us to *escape* from a dangerous situation that's already in motion, we might require at least 30 seconds of prior warning. For us to *defend* ourselves from a dangerous situation when it's too late for avoidance or escape, we'll still require at *least* several seconds of warning to find cover and/or draw our firearm. You can see pretty quickly that being unaware of our surroundings doesn't leave us with too many options.

OUTCOME	WARNING TIME	POSSIBLE RESULTS
Avoid	1 – 5+ Minutes	• You'll never know for the rest of your life whether or not you just avoided a violent crime or whether you overreacted. Personally, we can live with that. • If you were right about the situation, you've just gotten a "Get out of jail for free" card and possibly a "Get out of the hospital for free" card. • Your blood remains in your body where it belongs; your money remains in your bank where it belongs; and you'll remain at home with your family, where you belong.
Escape	30+ Seconds	• You've identified a dangerous situation in time to "exit stage left" before your options are limited to defend, but you're still in the middle of a bad situation.
Defend	3 – 5+ Seconds	• While you still have plenty of options other than "shoot the bad guy," you've now crossed a *significant* line where every action you are about to take will be second-guessed by the police, the media, the prosecuting attorney, and quite possibly a grand jury and jury. On the other hand, if it was your *only* choice, you do have a good chance of surviving. • Think about it this way–if you *knew* that the use of your firearm in self-defense would result in your incarceration (that's not a true legal test, but it is a good litmus test) and would cost you tens of thousands of dollars in legal expenses, how would that knowledge affect your decisions leading up to your use of force?

SITUATIONAL AWARENESS

So how do we gain those crucial seconds necessary to avoid or escape, or the few extra seconds that we'll need to find cover or draw our firearm if "defend" is the only option left to us?

A good start is to develop a keen sense of situational awareness. Like it sounds, situational awareness is an awareness of our immediate vicinity and of the people and objects within that environment. Being aware of our surroundings doesn't mean that we need to hire a reconnaissance team to scout out our shopping area in advance, but it *does* mean that we need to lift our heads up and observe more than just the cell phone in our hands while we text a message, or the few feet of sidewalk immediately in front of us.

"Smart" phones and MP3 players can cause us to focus our entire attention on a three–inch circle in front of us, making us oblivious to the rest of our environment.

Even without the distraction of an electronic device, too many people focus no farther than a circle of a few feet in front of them when they're in public.

Awareness Means 360°

When thinking about an awareness of our environment, we need to think about the 360 degree circle surrounding us, not just the individuals or objects to our front. When we move through public areas, we should think of a "bubble" surrounding us and our loved ones, and we need to be aware of everything and everyone inside of that bubble. Think about the way the secret service keeps a mobile bubble around the President of the United States. The secret service observes and categorizes everything within that bubble to identify any possible threat before it strikes. While we operate our own lives on a different scale, we can be no less vigilant—we are, in effect, our own bodyguards and first responders. Since we're lacking dozens of agents and overhead imagery, how do we go about monitoring that bubble around us? First off, it means that we need to lift our heads up from the sidewalk or our cell phones, and we need to watch where we're going. To get a 360 degree look at our surroundings, we'll need to use not only our peripheral vision (which provides about 180—200 degrees of visibility), but we'll also need to actually swivel our head to scan the area to our front, sides, and rear.

PERIPHERAL VISION

BLIND SPOT

We need to think of our immediate vicinity as having a "bubble" around it, and we need to be aware of everything and everyone in that bubble.

OUR PROTECTIVE "BUBBLE"

If you have a firearm and your attacker has a knife, you survive every time, right? Not necessarily. Lieutenant Dennis Tueller of the Salt Lake City Police Department demonstrated that simply having a firearm doesn't necessarily mean you could bring it into action in time to protect yourself, unless you closely observed threats (think situational awareness) within your protective bubble. Lieutenant Tueller observed that with practice, the average shooter could place two shots on target at a distance of 21 feet in about a second and a half. Tueller then ran another set of tests to determine exactly how quickly an "attacker" could cover that same distance, and discovered that it could be done in that same 1.5 seconds. Based on Tueller's experiment, most police departments in the U.S. now consider anything within 32–50 feet to be within the "danger zone," where an officer should be prepared to issue commands, increase distance, or gain access to a firearm.

THE TUELLER DRILL

1 **Version One**. With the defender armed with a blue or red replica gun and the "attacker" armed with a blue or red replica knife, this drill begins with the defender's replica gun holstered and the attacker 21 feet away. Without warning, the attacker charges the defender. The defender is successful if she can clear her replica gun from the holster and get it on "target" prior to the attacker touching her with the replica knife. Most individuals CANNOT bring their firearm on target in time.

2 **Version Two**. With instructor supervision, an outdoor range version of the drill can be run with the "attacker" and shooter positioned back-to-back. At the signal, the "attacker" runs away from the firing line and the shooter unholsters her gun and fires down range at a target 21 feet in front of her. The "attacker" stops as soon as the shot is fired. This exercise can help each individual calculate his or her own "danger zone."

We also need to actually *look* at the individuals in our immediate vicinity (including those behind us) to do two things. First, we want to make a quick assessment of the threat level of the individual; and second, we want to send the simple message, "I see you." That doesn't mean that we need to "eyeball" potential threats, and our look shouldn't signal, "I'm tougher than you" or, "I'm carrying a firearm." It simply needs to imply, "I see you."

This individual turns her head to observe anyone in her immediate area, and quickly makes eye contact to inform the individual, "I see you."

If we see something or someone who sets off our warning bells, we need to move away from the potential threat by slowing down, speeding up, changing direction, or turning around. If someone is approaching us from the rear, the "polite" reaction is to not turn around. We're not worried with polite. If we *do* hear (or otherwise sense) an individual behind us, we should turn to observe, and if the individual causes us concern, we should take evasive action by changing direction and observing his reaction, if any.

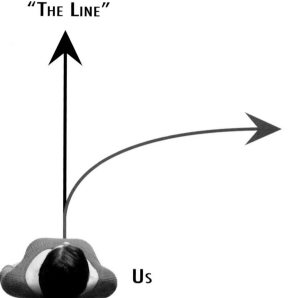

"THE LINE"

Us

To avoid a potential threat we may need to take evasive action, which might be as simple as "stepping off the line" by taking a right or left turn, then gauging your next move based upon the reaction. If the potential threat continues on "the line," then you can fall in step behind him. If he turns to follow you, then you need to increase your evasive action.

THE POTENTIAL THREAT

>> Regardless of how tough you might look on the outside, all a criminal will care about is whether you look like an easy victim. The truth is, an observant 110 pound woman is a less attractive victim than a 200 pound man who is entirely absorbed in his cell phone and is completely unaware of the attacker approaching from behind.

Not looking like a victim

When we observe our surroundings in this manner, it will be obvious to anyone watching us that we're being observant, and that fact alone will make us less attractive to potential assailants. We can increase that "unattractiveness" by walking with "purpose"—that is, we need to walk with our bodies erect and our heads up, and we should walk faster than the crowd, not slower. Imagine two individuals walking down the street—the first individual is walking with purpose, moving at a quick enough pace that she looks like she's going somewhere. That individual swivels her head to scan the area and she makes quick eye contact with any individual in her immediate area. The second individual is shuffling along at a slow pace, focused on a three-inch circle in front of him while he sends a text message on his cell phone. Which person do you think a criminal will want to target? When sizing up the first individual, the criminal will realize, "She's moving too fast and she saw me. She won't be easy to approach." On the other hand, he'll look at the second individual and think, "I can get right up on him, and he'll

never see me coming." Notice that we said nothing about the size or other characteristics of the potential "victims." The truth is, an observant 110 pound woman is a *less* attractive victim than a 200 pound man who is entirely absorbed in his cell phone and who is completely unaware of the attacker approaching from behind.

Finally, situational awareness shouldn't be thought of as something that needs to be "switched on," or as a chore. We personally make a game of it— when we're in public, we like to be people watchers, looking for a few different things. First, we like to challenge ourselves by trying to identify anyone else who might be carrying a firearm. It might be a slight bulge on the hip of another permit holder, or it might be the outline of a pistol grip under the shirt of a gang member, but that simple exercise ensures that we at least look at everyone around us. We watch hands, we watch eyes, and we pay extra close attention to people approaching or within our "danger zone." We also like to make a game of looking for individuals in condition white (more on that in the next section). In other words, we

Jeff Cooper

1920 – 2006

Father of the "Modern Technique" of Pistolcraft

Jeff Cooper's accomplishments include author, columnist, professor, and WWII and Korean War veteran. Cooper is also widely recognized as the Father of the "Modern Technique" of Pistolcraft, including the development of the four universal safety rules; updates and refinements to Jack Weaver's classic "Weaver Stance;" and development of the four "color codes" of awareness. In 1976, Cooper founded the Gunsite Academy in Paulden Arizona, which is still in operation today. Cooper died in September, 2006, and is sorely missed by thousands of students and fans.

like to look at things from the criminal's perspective. Next time you're in public, give it a try—look for individuals who are talking on their cell phones or texting and are completely absorbed by that task (and completely unaware of their surroundings). Watch for people who shuffle along slower than the crowd around them, looking as if they're going nowhere. One of our favorites (or biggest pet peeves) is observing people who walk down the middle of the driving lanes in parking lots or parking garages, and are completely unaware that a vehicle weighing several thousand pounds is bearing down on them. If they're not aware that a 5,000 pound truck is behind them, do you think they'll notice if a 170-pound rapist is sneaking up behind them? Finally, take the time to monitor yourself—how often do you find yourself out in public, immersed in a cell phone call and oblivious to your surroundings? How often do you discover that you're tailgating the only other vehicle on the freeway, when two or three other lanes are clear? To hone our situational awareness skills, we like to use the color codes of awareness developed by the late Jeff Cooper.

The "Color Codes"

Originally developed by the U.S. Marines in the Pacific during World War II to help mentally condition Marines to prepare for an attack, the Color Codes were later modified by Colonel Jeff Cooper for use in educating civilians to help us to become more aware of our surroundings, and to not only prepare for violent encounters, but if possible, to avoid them in the first place.

On the following pages, we've detailed what type of mental awareness we should have at each level, and what our actions might be. We've also included a quote from Jeff Cooper with his thoughts on each level of awareness.

> **"** *My advice isn't for everyone. It's primarily for legally armed citizens who refuse to be victims.* **"**
> **Colonel Jeff Cooper**

>> If you live your life in a perpetual state of "condition white," you have a
high probability of eventually finding yourself in "condition red."

Unaware

In Condition White, you are unaware of what's going on around you.

» You don't think anything bad will happen and may believe that violent crime happens to "other people."

» Modern technologies such as cell phones, smart phones, and MP3 players create a perfect environment to lull individuals into condition white, allowing criminals to approach within inches of their potential victim, making avoidance or escape nearly impossible.

» Individuals in condition white often fail to recognize emotions or aggressiveness in others and they might enter into arguments without realizing that they've moved beyond what's safe, or they might believe that they can talk their way out of trouble. They will also be unaware when they've strayed into unsafe areas such as poorly lit areas, areas with blind spots, or areas away from the crowds; or they might put themselves into unsafe situations by allowing their gas tank to go to "E" or forgetting where they parked their car.

» It's the condition of most victims, and it's the condition that criminals look for.

» You should never allow yourself to be in condition white when armed, because your ability to avoid or escape a dangerous situation is compromised—that means that a defensive shooting might occur when it could have been avoided!

> 66 *If attacked in this state the only thing that may save you is the inadequacy and ineptitude of your attacker. When confronted by something nasty your reaction will probably be, 'Oh my God! This can't be happening to me'.* 99
>
> **Colonel Jeff Cooper**

Unaware
This individual is preoccupied with her MP3 player, and is *completely unaware* of her surroundings.

Aware

In Condition Yellow, you are aware of your surroundings.

» This is the condition you should be in any time you're in public.

» You are aware of what's happening in the immediate vicinity, and you proceed with caution.

» You are not paranoid or overreactive, but you keep an eye out for potential threats and their sources.

» Your posture, eyes, and demeanor say, "I am alert" and you walk faster than the crowd.

» You should become comfortable with simple habits such as scanning an area (rooms, street corners, etc.) before entering; and identifying exits and cover wherever you are.

» You make brief eye contact with individuals in your immediate area, letting them know, "I see you."

» Individuals in condition yellow have developed safe habits such as avoiding arguments, identifying everyone and everything within their protective "bubble" (including objects that can work to their benefit such as cover, barriers, and exits), and following the conflict avoidance ideas outlined in this chapter.

» If you are armed, you must be in yellow.

> "*Relaxed alert. No specific threat situation. Your mindset is that 'today could be the day I may have to defend myself.' You are simply aware that the world is an unfriendly place and that you are prepared to do something if necessary. You use your eyes and ears. You don't have to be armed in this state but if you are armed you should be in Condition Yellow. You should always be in Yellow whenever you are in unfamiliar surroundings or among people you don't know.*"

Colonel Jeff Cooper

Aware
This individual is aware of her surroundings and is not distracting herself with any electronic device. She not only observes the area to her front, she also swivels her head to look to her sides and directly behind her. She makes momentary eye contact with anyone within her protective "bubble."

Heightened Awareness

In Condition Orange, you have identified a possible threat or threats. This is a heightened state of awareness.

» You realize that something *may* be wrong.

» There *may* be a danger to yourself or others.

» You make a plan on how to react, including identifying cover, barriers, or an exit strategy.

» You may begin to take preemptive action such as turning around, stepping off "the line," increasing your distance, or making simple, direct verbal commands such as, "Stay back!" or, "Don't come any closer!"

» You decide on a mental "trigger" that will move you to take action, such as an individual refusing your verbal commands and moving closer into your "bubble."

» You mentally prepare yourself for a confrontation or a rapid escape.

» You may begin to feel the effects of adrenaline or other automated responses described in our physiological section in Chapter Five.

» Your pistol may remain holstered, but you should prepare to access it, such as brushing aside outer clothing; putting your hand in the pocket where you have your firearm in a pocket holster; or reaching into your purse and getting a tight grip on the pistol.

" *Specific alert. Something is not quite right and has gotten your attention. Your radar has picked up a specific alert. You shift your primary focus to determine if there is a threat. In Condition Orange, you set a mental trigger. If the threat proves to be nothing, you shift back to Condition Yellow.* "

Colonel Jeff Cooper

Heightened Awareness

This individual has sensed or observed something or someone that causes her concern, and she takes preemptive action by taking cover. She closely observes the situation to determine if there is a threat, and makes a plan on how to react. Even if she can't definitively categorize the situation as an actual threat, she may decide to avoid the situation entirely and take evasive action by walking, running, or driving away.

Action

In Condition Red, action is immediate.

» Your mental trigger has been tripped and you execute your plan, either to escape, take cover, or engage the threat.

» Trust your instincts—it's better to run away from a situation that turned out *not* to be a threat than it is to get stuck in a mental block of, "This can't be what I think it is," and guessing wrong.

» Instinct and adrenaline will cause involuntary reactions and *must* be calculated into your training program (See the section on the physiological reaction to stress in Chapter Five.) You should expect your hands to tremble and your fine motor skills to degrade.

» If engaging the threat, operate within the rules governing the use of force, including the obligation to retreat if possible, and the obligation to use something less than deadly force if it will suffice. See Chapter Four for a full definition of your obligations and rights when it comes to a use of force to defend yourself.

» A use of force is *not* the required outcome. If you've closely observed the immediate area and have identified an escape route, retreat may be the most logical and prudent course of action.

> 66 *Condition Red is (action). Your mental trigger has been tripped (established back in Condition Orange). The mental trigger will differ depending upon the circumstances. Whatever trigger is selected, it is a button that once pushed, results in immediate action on your part.* 99

Colonel Jeff Cooper

Action: Expose Firearm
In this example, the individual makes the attacker aware that she is armed and is ready to defend herself.

Action: Escape
In this example, the individual has identified a threat early enough to make a rapid escape or to head toward cover.

Action: Draw Firearm and Issue Commands
In this example, the individual forcefully issues commands with her firearm at a low ready position (and the finger outside the trigger guard).

Action: Engage the Threat
In this example, the individual points her firearm at the attacker and is ready to take whatever action is required to stop the threat.

IS ACTION FASTER THAN REACTION?

If an attacker unexpectedly lunges at you with a knife, can you draw your firearm in time to stop him? Can you "out draw" an attacker if he already has a firearm pointed at you? When the threat ends, how quickly can you stop shooting? Is there any plausible explanation for why an attacker might be shot in the back? These hypothetical situations all beg the question, "Is action faster than reaction?" or better yet, "Just how important is situational awareness, *really?*"

To help answer the questions posed above (and to help you understand the limits of human reaction time), we're going to take a look at two studies which analyzed reaction times to visual stimuli. The first study analyzed braking reaction time, while the second study analyzed the reaction time required for shooters to start shooting, and to stop shooting.

Braking: How Long Does it Take to Stop?

Before we delve into reaction times of responsibly armed citizens defending themselves from attack, let's take a look at a study analyzing the reaction times of drivers to a braking maneuver. In the article, *How Long Does It Take To Stop? Methodological Analysis of Driver Perception-Brake Times* published in 2000, researchers concluded that "reaction time" was actually a sequence of multiple stages. For our purposes, we'll group them into the following components:

» *Perception/Cognitive Processing Time.* This is the time required for the individual to receive, recognize, and process the sensory signal (auditory, visual, etc.), and to formulate a response.

» *Motor Reaction Time.* This is the time required for the individual to perform the required movement, such as lifting the foot off the accelerator and applying the brake.

We've all tried the "dollar bill" trick, where one individual drops a dollar bill without warning, and a second person tries grabbing it. The question is, why is it so difficult to catch the dollar, even though we're expecting it to be dropped? As shown in the studies outlined in this section, researchers know that even when a stimulus is expected, humans require between one-quarter and one-half of a second to perceive and process the input, and on average, another .06 seconds to complete even the simplest movements such as pressing a trigger, or pinching our fingers to catch a dollar bill. In the "dollar bill" trick, gravity beats reaction time, since even the fastest reaction time of .31 seconds results in the dollar bill falling just over a foot and a half before the brain can process the input, and the fingers can pinch closed.

Although you may be perfectly within your rights to walk down a dark alley all alone, you've already made two mistakes. This individual might be looking for a handout, or he might be looking for your money or your life. Fix your mistakes before it's too late by turning around and returning as quickly as possible to a crowded area.

Low Light Areas

Darkness is a criminal's friend. Back entrances of homes or businesses, dark alleys, parking areas with burned out lights; these are all areas where criminals may hover when looking for easy victims. Especially dangerous are areas with a rapid transition from bright lights to low light or darkness. It takes our eyes as long as 20 minutes to adapt to low light, and criminals who are stalking victims in these areas will be well adapted to the low light while our eyes are still adjusting. The parking garage on the opposite page is a good example—the garage contains plenty of well lit areas, but it also contains an area of low light, which should be avoided. When parking in a garage such as this, you should pick a spot that allows you to walk through the well lit areas in order to get to your destination, rather than a spot that requires you to walk through the areas with burned out lights. If a criminal is in the area looking for a victim, he's much more likely to hover behind a vehicle or pillar in the dark areas, than in the brightly-lit areas.

Barriers, Concealment, and Cover

When under threat, any barrier between you and the threat increases your ability to escape or evade the attack. Vehicles, tables, chairs, even a display case at a convenience store can help to foil an attacker with an edged or impact weapon. Concealment is anything that hides you from the threat (a closed door, a wall, or anything you can duck behind) while cover (things like concrete pillars, or the front of vehicles where the engine block is) protects you from incoming bullets. As part of your situational awareness when in public, you'll need to be aware of these objects within your environment, and make a mental note on how they can help to serve as barriers, concealment, or cover.

Escape Routes

In addition to looking for barriers, concealment, and cover, you should also identify at least two escape routes wherever you are, in case you need to quickly put distance between yourself and a threat. You'll recall from our topic on "Condition Orange," that if a situation doesn't feel right, you can choose to exit the area preemptively, even if you haven't positively identified a threat. If you *have* positively identified a threat, having identified escape routes in advance can save valuable time, when seconds will count. In particular, when under the threat of a firearm, you'll need to spoil your attacker's aim by increasing your distance as quickly as possible. Picture how the difficulty increases at your local range when you increase the distance between you and the target from 10 feet to 50 feet to 100 feet. How about pushing it out to 100, 200, or 300 feet? The attacker will find it just as aggravating.

Cover
Behind engine blocks
and concrete pillars.

Exit Strategy
Out of garage or back to
mall.

Area to Avoid
Where lights
are burned out.

>> According to FBI statistics, burglars enter the front door of homes 34% of the time, and back or screen doors 22% of the time. The most common method of breaching the door? A good, swift kick. To test the security effectiveness of locks and doors, Consumer Reports has established a standard test, using a 100-pound battering ram capable of delivering varying degrees of force to the door. In a test conducted by the DIY Network's show Deconstruction®, a variety of door locks were tested to determine how long it would take to breach the door using the average strength of a kick. When testing a standard deadbolt and strike plate with standard length screws, the door was breached after just two impacts of the battering ram, at just 60 joules per "kick." When tested using the same dead bolt, but a reinforced strikeplate ($10 – $15) and three-inch screws, the door was breached only after 13 impacts, at an average of 160 joules each, which equates to more than 17-times the force required to breach the standard door and lock.

HOME SECURITY

Students of self-defense can spend hours or days studying and training on methods of staying safe in public, including perfecting the skills of situational awareness and the use of a handgun in self-defense. Yet those same individuals can exhibit sloppy and unsafe behavior when it comes to securing the one place where we *should* feel safe, namely our homes. One reason for this disparity may simply be that when we're in our homes, our places of sanctuary, it becomes easy to slip back into "condition white" and to believe that nothing bad can occur. Another reason may be that it's more difficult to quantify the dangers of a home invasion when compared to the risks of other crimes of violence. While the FBI maintains detailed crime data in their Uniform Crime Report (the source for most media reports on violent crime) including the crime of burglary, they do *not* differentiate between burglaries that occur in empty homes versus occupied homes. If a violent crime occurred during a home invasion, the FBI would categorize the crime under *two* headings such as burglary and rape, but with no separate category of "home invasion," it's impossible to determine, nationally or locally, just how common these "hot burglaries" are using the FBI data alone. Suffice to say, taking personal responsibility for our own safety, and the safety of our families, *cannot* stop at the front door.

Thinking Like a Criminal

When evaluating the security of your home, we suggest putting yourself in the mind of the criminal who wants to gain access to your home, and conducting a thorough inspection, inside and out. You should start from the outside of the home and make a methodical, 360-degree inspection starting from the ground up. During your inspection, you'll need to ask yourself the types of questions we've posed on the opposite page.

Home Security Inspection Checklist

Windows:

- Identify all windows that are on the ground level that could potentially allow a home invader to fit through. Never mind determining if it would be *easy* for the home invader to do so; they've been known to do some pretty unorthodox things to gain entry to a home.

- Do they lock properly?

- Are they locked?

- Does anything block the view of the window from the outside such as a tree or shrubs?

- Is there anything outside the house that could potentially be used as a step stool to climb through the window? While home invaders aren't likely to carry their own ladder or step stool, they *will* take advantage of anything you've left outside that will make their job easier.

- Do you have alarm company stickers on your windows? New, fresh looking stickers—not stickers that look like they were put on by the previous occupant.

- Do your windows have plastic or metal locks?

- If you have standard hung windows, do you have a secondary security device, such as a bar stop?

- If you have casement windows, do you have standard or reinforced hinges?

- Do the windows have a protective laminate applied to the inside of the window, or baked inside? In other words, will your windows be shattered with a single blow, or are they designed to withstand repeated blows?

- On the first floor, what's in front of the windows? For example, are they blocked by a table or other barrier that a home invader would need to climb over, or is the area wide open?

Doors:

- What is the quality and strength of the front, back, side, and interior garage doors? It's natural to focus on the strength of your *front* door, but criminals will focus on whichever door is the weakest.

- What's the general appearance of the door? Does it look new, or is it old, faded, and looking primed for a good kick?

- Are the hinges on the outside or inside?

- Do you have an ability to see who is at the door without them seeing you?

- Do you use a deadbolt, chain lock, or throw-over lock?

- How long are the screws that are used to mount the strike plate? You'll actually need to unscrew the screws to answer this question.

Lights:

- Is your house well lit, or poorly lit on all sides? How about the adjoining neighbors' houses? Criminals will not only look for dark homes, they'll look for dark homes, *surrounded* by dark homes.

General Appearance:

- How close are trees or shrubs to your home? Is there anything that a criminal can hide behind while trying to enter a window or door?

- Do you have burglar alarm signs (in new condition) at all entry points?

Alarm:

- Do you have a security alarm, and do you set it? (Homes that have alarms are *three times* less likely to be burglarized.)

- Is it connected to an alarm service?

- Do you have motion detectors, glass break sensors, and sensors on the windows?

Making Your Home More Secure

Once you've completed a security inspection of your home, it's time to look at methods to make your home more secure. In the recommendations which follow, we've offered a variety of solutions costing just a few dollars at the low-end, to several thousand dollars at the high-end. The great news is that even the lowest cost solutions will dramatically decrease the probability that your home will be subject to a burglary or home invasion.

Windows

» Replace any plastic locks with metal locks (about $2.50 each), and add a bar stop to each window ($20).

» Treat the inside of windows with a plastic window treatment (the type of treatment used to insulate the windows), which will dramatically increase the effort required to break through the window (about $6.50 per square foot).

» If you're *serious* about window security, invest in replacement casement windows with a reinforced hinge, metal locks, and a protective laminate that's baked into the window (about $350 per window).

Doors

» Replace any doors that are not steel or solid core, including the door interior to the garage. Choose a door that doesn't contain clear windows that would allow a person outside the home to see in; instead, add your own hotel-style peephole ($6 – $11).

» All exterior doors should have a deadbolt and/or a throw-over type lock (about $15).

» Replace standard strike plates with reinforced strike plates, and use extra deep screws (at least three-inches long) which will anchor into the wall stud, rather than just the door frame ($12—$15).

» If you're serious about door security, invest in a high-security lock ($180 or more), which defeats criminal's ability to use a "bump key" to pick the lock. High security locks use a unique pin configuration and hardened cylinders, which require 30—40 minutes to defeat, even for a trained locksmith.

» If you're *really* serious about door security, invest in a solid steel door from Master Security (from $500 to several thousand dollars), which have five built-in deadbolts and an anti-pick lock. Master Security doors are designed to stop sledgehammer blows and even gunfire. In a test on the DIY Network's show Deconstruction®, four sledgehammer armed testers failed to breach the door even after ten minutes of repeated blows.

Exterior

» Add exterior lights to all sides of the house, including the sides not containing doors. If you're concerned about electricity costs, put them on a motion detector circuit. Additional lights throughout the front and back yard will encourage a potential criminal to move further down the street to find a house that isn't so well lit.

» As mentioned, FBI statistics confirm that about 56% of home entries are through the front door or back door, and those same statistics show that first floor windows are the next favored entry point at about 23%. In another Deconstruction® test, five different types of windows with varying security mechanisms were tested to determine how well they'd withstand a determined home invader or burglar. The testers discovered that a standard hung window with a single lock could be breached in less than a minute by breaking the lock, or in seconds by breaking the glass. Same for a basic casement window. By adding a bar stop ($20) and a plastic window treatment ($6.50 per square foot) to the standard hung window; or reinforced hinges to the casement window, the time to breach the window was increased dramatically. For real security, consider upgrading to high-security casement windows with reinforced hinges and metal locks, which also come with a protective laminate that's baked directly into the glass. Even after repeated strikes with a crowbar, the window failed to break during the Deconstruction® test. The cost? About $375 per window. The peace of mind? Priceless.

» As much as you might love the bushes and trees that have been growing around your house for years, if they're overgrown, they're going to provide cover for someone trying to break into your house, or lying in wait for you while you approach the door. Trim all bushes at least four-feet from the house, and trim any tree branch that blocks the view to your windows or doors.

» Place new alarm company signs at all doors, and stickers on all first floor windows.

Burglar Alarm

The first step in effectively using a burglar alarm, is to get the alarm. The second step is to set it, religiously. Insurance company surveys have shown that 60%—81% of people who have burglar alarms fail to set them when at home, or even when on vacation. The number one excuse (53%) for failing to set the alarm is because the homeowner leaves pets indoors, however, alarm manufacturers now offer "pet immune" motion detectors. By combining an infrared scanner with a motion detector, the systems are able to differentiate between the heat of a pet, and the heat of an intruder. In addition to the new "pet immune" features, security systems themselves have evolved from clunky systems requiring hard wiring at doors and windows (and slow law enforcement responses as alarm companies initiated "call backs" to determine if the alarm was an actual emergency or a false alarm), to state of the art systems like

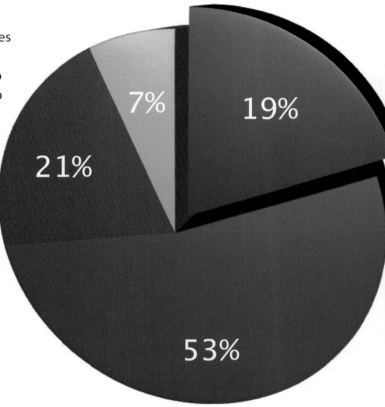

● Set Alarm
● Don't Set Because of Pets
● Don't Set Because of Children
● Forget to Set

something out of a spy novel. Two-way systems are now available from companies such as AlarmForce®, which immediately opens a live channel between the home and the monitoring service when the alarm goes off. This allows the customer service agent to immediately differentiate between an actual emergency and a false alarm. Systems are also available with "glass break" detectors, which are more effective than simple window monitors that only sound if the window is opened (but wouldn't sound if the window was broken). The detectors are even tuned to differentiate between the sound of a broken window, and the sound of a broken glass.

Planning for Home Defense

In addition to taking steps to better secure our homes, we'll also need to take steps to plan for what to do if all of our security measures fail, and we still find ourselves in the middle of a home invasion. While you don't necessarily need to draw a floor layout of your home as part of your home invasion plan, you should at least *have* a plan and discuss it with everyone in your household, including your children.

Think of this as no different than discussing a plan in case of fire, tornado, hurricane, or earthquake. When discussing a home invasion plan with the family, we'd suggest reviewing the checklist items on the following page, and ensuring that all family members are aware of how to dial 911, and all age-appropriate family members are aware of the location of the home defense firearm and how to use it. Plan a route for all family members to head to the most secure areas of the home, and include in the plan who will get the phone and dial 911, who will access the defensive firearm, and who will assist loved ones.

In addition to planning for actively defending the home, we also suggest that you plan for retreat or escape, even if you're not legally obligated to do so.

» Home security systems have evolved from clunky systems requiring hard wiring at doors and windows, and slow law enforcement responses as alarm companies initiated "call backs" to determine if the alarm was an actual emergency or a false alarm, to state of the art systems like something out of a spy novel. Two-way systems are now available from companies such as AlarmForce®, which immediately opens a live channel between the home and the monitoring service when the alarm goes off. This allows the customer service agent to immediately differentiate between an actual emergency and a false alarm. Systems are also available with "glass break" detectors, which are more effective than simple window monitors that only sound if the window is opened. The detectors are even tuned to differentiate between the sound of a broken window, and a broken glass. For pet owners, ADT® and other manufacturers now offer "pet immune" motion detectors. By combining an infrared scanner with the motion detector, the systems are able to differentiate between the heat of a pet, and the heat of an intruder.

For example, if you needed to quickly retreat from a room or from the home, what are the options? What rooms are the safest, and what doors are the closest? If you exit the house, in which direction do you run to find the closest neighbor? You can include older children as active participants in the plan by assigning them with simple tasks that can help keep themselves and their siblings safe. For example, their tasks could include:

» Get out of the house and find a neighbor, and ask the neighbor to call 911.
» Get the younger kids into the same bedroom, and close and barricade the door.

We suggest two or three small points for each child, such as, "If something bad happens, your job is to get out of the house, get to a neighbor, and have him or her call 911. Then your job is done."

Finally, it's important to discuss what *not* to do in the event of a home invasion. For example, if everyone in the family is in the same part of the house, then it is not necessary, prudent, or smart to "clear rooms" looking for the intruder. In addition, it's extremely important to discuss what to do if a family member is coming home late or unexpectedly, and how to communicate it if a guest will be in the home. The use of a family "code word" or "challenge and reply" can avoid tragedy if your teenage son or daughter has decided to sneak a significant other into the house for a late night rendezvous, or if your spouse has gotten up for a late night snack.

The Home Defense Checklist

- Are the front and back lights on?
- Is the alarm on?
- Are all doors locked (including deadbolt and/or throw-over lock)?
- Is the home defense firearm in its proper location and is it loaded? (Keep in mind that you'll need to follow federal and state safe storage laws.)
- Where is the phone and how do I dial 911 (in the dark, with a head full of cobwebs)?
- If the home is invaded, what room do we move to?
- If we need to exit the home, which neighbor's house do we go to?
- What commands do we give?
- How do I identify a friend from a foe?
- What's a family code word to identify whom and where you are?
- How do we inform our family that we'll be coming home late, or that a guest will be in the home?
- Does each family member know how to dial 911?
- Does each age-appropriate family member know how to use the home defense firearm?
- What do we do when the police arrive?

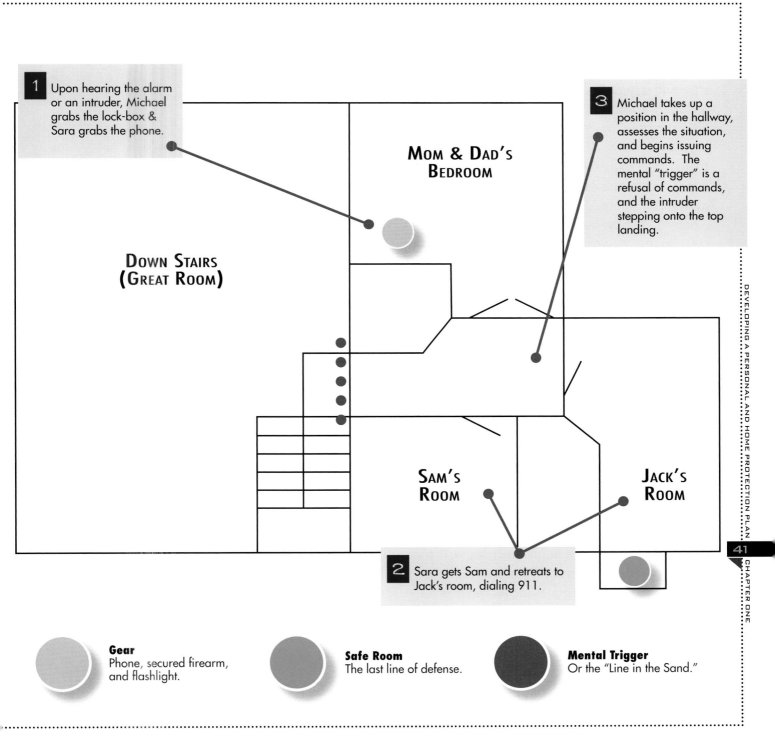

1 Upon hearing the alarm or an intruder, Michael grabs the lock-box & Sara grabs the phone.

MOM & DAD'S BEDROOM

3 Michael takes up a position in the hallway, assesses the situation, and begins issuing commands. The mental "trigger" is a refusal of commands, and the intruder stepping onto the top landing.

DOWN STAIRS (GREAT ROOM)

SAM'S ROOM

JACK'S ROOM

2 Sara gets Sam and retreats to Jack's room, dialing 911.

Gear
Phone, secured firearm, and flashlight.

Safe Room
The last line of defense.

Mental Trigger
Or the "Line in the Sand."

MENTAL EXERCISES

With enough time and money, dozens of advanced shooting schools are available to the average citizen, including advanced topics such as force-on-force, low light shooting, shoot/no-shoot scenarios, etc. In fact, we're sure that a school exists that would teach us to use infrared gear, rappel from a helicopter, breach doors, and rescue hostages, but let's face it—the average permit holder is lucky to get to the range once a month. So how do we bridge the gap between the training that we *do* perform, versus the type of scenario we might find ourselves in if a critical incident does occur? One simple alternative we can do while sitting in our armchair at home is to run through a series of mental exercises.

Paranoia?

Mental exercises shouldn't be confused with paranoia, or with a responsibly armed citizen fantasizing about getting in a shootout with a bad guy. It's simply a process to have a mental checklist of items that wouldn't normally be part of our time on the range. For example, when walking through a parking garage, picture what you would do if someone stepped out from behind a car with a knife. What commands would you give? Where would you find cover? What would be your mental trigger? At home, mentally walk through the step-by-step process that you would go through if you heard the front door being kicked down. These simple mental exercises can help to avoid the, "Oh my God" reaction described by Cooper.

On the Range

Mental exercises can extend to our time on the range as well. One goal of mental exercises on the range may seem counterintuitive, which is to elevate our stress level to the point that our body will generate higher levels of adrenaline. This might be done by converting a relaxed round of shooting at 21-feet to an exercise where we imagine the target is an attacker, charging us with a knife. The goal should be to place several rounds into critical areas within one to two seconds (the time it would take for the attacker to reach us). The results might be lower accuracy when compared to a more relaxed practice round, but it will force us to learn to shoot safely and accurately, while having a pounding heart and shaking hands. When running mental exercises at home or at the range, you'll need to create hypothetical problems (such as the examples on the opposite page) that require a solution. Your solution will need to be a *complete* solution; that is, it should include the checklist items on the opposite page, including evaluating your options and preparing for the aftermath.

At Home:

» What if I hear the front door being kicked down, or a window shattered?

» What if my burglar alarm goes off in the middle of the night?

» What if a stranger at the door suddenly produces a weapon?

» What should I do if I hear someone outside of the house?

» What if I believe they're stealing my property? (This is an easy one—stay inside, call 911, and be a good witness.)

» What if I find the door to my house open upon arriving home? (Also an easy one—stay outside, call 911, and let the police do their job.)

» What if I hear someone in the house at night? How do I distinguish a family member from an intruder?

In Public:

» What if I'm approached by one or more individuals who cause me concern?

» What if I "step off the line" and they follow me?

» What do I do if they produce a weapon? What if it's a knife? What if it's a gun?

» What if a threat materializes between a loved one and me?

» What if I see an attack in progress on someone else?

» If I see someone that I believe has committed, or is about to commit a crime, what should I do? Should I follow them, or stay in a safe location and call 911?

Mental Exercise Checklist

- What are my options?
- What cover or barriers are available?
- How do I move "off the line?"
- How do I draw from the holster?
- What commands do I give?
- What are the requirements for speed versus accuracy?
- How do I work the physiological reactions into my response?

- How do I disengage/re-engage any safety devices including holster retention, manual safeties, or decockers?
- How do I clear a malfunction?
- How do I perform a reload?
- What do I do in the aftermath?
- Whom do I call and what do I say?
- What do I say to the police when they arrive?
- What will I do when I'm arrested?
- Where is my lawyer's contact information?

HOW DOES A CONCEALED CARRY PERMIT FIT?

When it comes to our personal protection plans, a "Concealed Carry Permit" simply provides us with one more option that might be used if we find ourselves unable to avoid or escape from a dangerous situation when out in public. But, as discussed on the opposite page, possessing a firearm actually *elevates* our legal and moral need to find ways to avoid or escape. A concealed carry permit should *not* be confused with any additional authority under the law, beyond the right to carry an object in public that might otherwise be illegal. In most of our experiences, the only individuals that we've known who have carried firearms on a daily basis have been law enforcement (who *do* have additional authority), so it's understandable that confusion can occur about what exactly our permit authorizes us to do. First, let's look at some things that our permit is *not*.

What a Permit is Not

An Invincibility Shield

We cannot look at our concealed carry permit as a permit to go to places, do things, or say things that we shouldn't otherwise. If we ignore the guidelines on conflict avoidance and allow ourselves to be placed in a dangerous situation that we could have avoided, we'll quickly discover that our permit does not stop incoming bullets, and it will *not* shield us from an aggressive prosecutor who believes that we were spoiling for a fight.

A Shield of ANY Kind

Never confuse a concealed carry permit with a "Junior Police Officer" badge. Police have specific responsibilities (such as chasing down bad guys) that could put us in legal peril if we tried to imitate them. For example, if we tried to prevent a property crime (such as attempting to stop someone from breaking into a car, or chasing down a purse thief), or if we followed an individual who we suspected was up to no good and the situation escalated to the point where we used force to protect ourselves, the prosecutor could argue that we've broken one or more of the rules governing the use of force or deadly force outlined in Chapter Four, and we may be charged with a crime. On the same topic, we'll occasionally hear of an enterprising organization selling "Concealed Carry Permit" badges, modeled after police badges. These are *really* bad ideas, not only because they could be confused with actual police badges (possibly resulting in a charge of impersonating a police officer) but they may also give the "holder" of the badge the incorrect impression that they have some special powers or authority. Save your money.

A "Fix" For Bad Attitudes

If you pull out your handgun and wave it at someone in an attempt to adjust his behavior (such as the guy who just cut you off in traffic), you'll quickly find yourself on your way to jail, charged with assault or worse.

SO WHAT'S IT GOOD FOR?

A concealed carry permit is just that—it's a permit to carry an object in public that might otherwise be illegal. *Every other law* that applies to non-permit holders also applies to us, including the rules governing the use of force and deadly force. In fact, our permit may put us in greater legal jeopardy compared to non-permit holders, since many state and federal statutes provide additional penalties when a firearm falls into the mix. For example, if a non-permit holder verbally threatens someone with death or great bodily harm for cutting him off in traffic, he might be charged with misdemeanor assault. Insert a permit holder and a firearm into the same situation, and he should expect to be charged with felony assault, and anything else the prosecutor can come up with.

» If you're unlucky enough to see this charming fellow in the lane next to you, keep calm, don't react, and keep that middle finger to yourself.

SELF–DEFENSE FIREARM BASICS

Self-defense firearm basics should be an enjoyable topic for new and experienced shooters alike. In this chapter we'll start by reviewing what are called the "Universal Safety Rules" that are non-negotiable when it comes to safe firearm ownership, handling, and use. We'd love to say that the universal rules were our idea, but that's not the case. Like the color codes of awareness, the Universal Safety Rules were developed by Colonel Jeff Cooper and have been adopted by nearly every firearms training organization in the world. We'll also cover a number of other safety considerations that are part of safe firearm ownership including topics associated with firearm maintenance, safety on the range, and safety considerations when selecting

a holster. We'll also cover the proper clearance (unloading) procedures for both semi-automatics and revolvers, including lots of good pictures to help you through the process.

In this chapter, we'll also explain the difference between double action and single action handguns. This might sound like kind of a technical topic, but it's an important one to understand because it not only affects the operation of your firearm, it's an important safety consideration when selecting a firearm. In our example, we'll be using a pistol called a SIG Sauer P229 (for you Cliff Clavins, that's the same pistol used by U.S. Air Marshals), but the theory is the same for both semi-autos and revolvers. Once we're through that topic, we'll be reviewing several different types of revolvers and semi-autos. Revolvers have been a mainstay of repeating handguns since Sam Colt developed the first modern design in 1836 with his Colt Patterson model. More than 175 years later, Colt would still recognize today's modern revolvers as having many of the same functional components as his designs, although he'd probably find them a bit less attractive than his beauties. As you'll see in our examples, revolvers have a revolving cylinder, which typically has between five and eight chambers, each capable of holding a cartridge.

Semi-automatics have been on the market since the late 1890s, but it took another famous inventor, John Moses Browning, to perfect the design with his Model 1911 (which was adopted by the U.S. Army as its standard sidearm in March of 1911). Having celebrated its 100th birthday, the 1911 is now produced by more than 15 manufacturers

and remains one of the most popular handguns made. We've included a walkthrough of the 1911, as well as three other semi-autos, including the Glock, the Springfield XD(M), and the SIG Sauer P250. We'll even help explain how these gadgets work with a step-by-step cutaway of what happens when you press the trigger.

Also included in this chapter are introductions to the home defense shotgun and the AR-15, including what options or features you should consider if picking out either of these platforms for home defense; plus, a short explanation of how Tasers and pepper spray works.

THE UNIVERSAL SAFETY RULES

By itself, a firearm is an inert object. By itself, it doesn't just "go off." Insert a human being and a negligent discharge can occur when the proper safety rules aren't followed. The following safety rules were developed by Jeff Cooper and must be followed whether at home, on the range, or carrying in public. All firearm "accidents" can be eliminated by following these easy to remember rules.

Rule #1: Treat all guns as though they are always loaded and always perform a clearance check every time you pick one up! Most firearm "accidents" occur with firearms that the users had sworn were unloaded. Never, never, *never* grow careless with a firearm. Every single time you pick it up, perform the proper clearance procedure and educate those in your household how to do the same. Treat a firearm that you've just unloaded with the *exact* same respect as one that you've just loaded.

Rule #2: Never point your gun at anything that you are not willing to destroy! While your firearm has to point somewhere, you should always ensure that it's pointed in a direction that can serve as a backstop if the firearm were to discharge. A good method to practice this rule is to pretend that a laser extends out from the end of the barrel. You should NEVER let that imaginary beam touch anything that won't stop a bullet (that includes any wall, ceiling, or floor that could not stop a bullet) or ANYONE (that includes your own hands, legs, or body) unless you are in a defensive situation and all criteria is present for the use of deadly force.

Rule #3: Keep your finger OFF the trigger and outside the trigger guard until you are on target and have made the decision to shoot! Until these criteria are met, your trigger finger should be straight and placed firmly on the frame of the

Until you are on target and have made the decision to shoot, your finger should be straight, and placed firmly on the frame of the firearm, outside of the triggerguard.

firearm. In a defensive situation, do NOT put your finger in the trigger guard unless all requirements have been met for the use of deadly force. Training consistently with this method will avoid a negligent discharge in a stress situation, when your body's natural adrenaline dump will cause the strength of your grip to increase.

Rule #4: Always be sure of your target and beyond! Said another way, you must POSITIVELY identify your target before you shoot and you MUST be convinced that anything that you shoot at (a target on the range, or an attacker in a parking garage) must have an effective backstop to stop your bullet, otherwise you MUST NOT SHOOT!

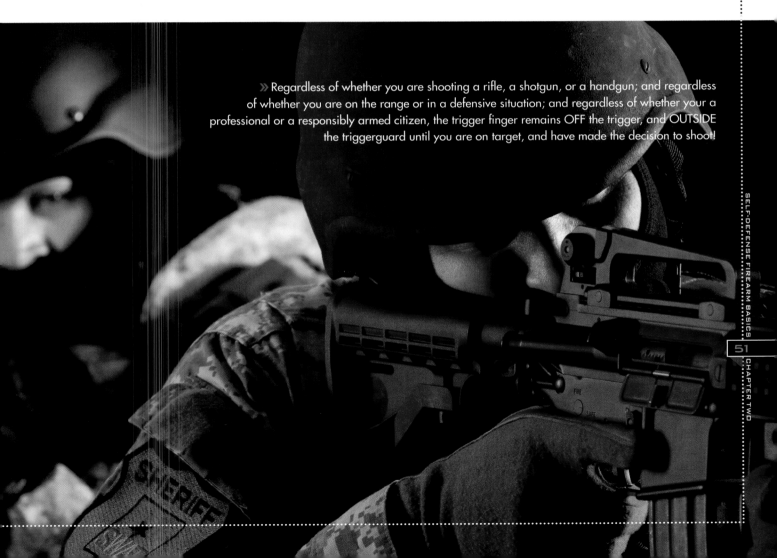

» Regardless of whether you are shooting a rifle, a shotgun, or a handgun; and regardless of whether you are on the range or in a defensive situation; and regardless of whether your a professional or a responsibly armed citizen, the trigger finger remains OFF the trigger, and OUTSIDE the triggerguard until you are on target, and have made the decision to shoot!

CLEARING SEMI-AUTOMATICS

As mentioned in Universal Safety Rule #1, we *always* do a clearance procedure *anytime* we pick up a firearm (other than the exceptions noted below). This might seem a bit ridiculous (as in "I *just* cleared the pistol, why would I clear it again?") but this habit will ensure that you avoid the, "I thought it was unloaded" type of accident. During the clearance procedures that follow, always remember all four Universal Safety Rules, including maintaining muzzle control and keeping your finger OUTSIDE of the trigger guard.

The *only* exceptions to this rule are: When operating on a "hot" range and picking up a previously loaded firearm from the benchrest in preparation to fire; when retrieving a loaded handgun from a gun vault to holster it for the day; or, when placing a loaded handgun in a gun vault at the end of the day.

Properly clearing a semi-automatic takes four steps. Clearing a revolver? Just two steps.

1 Drop the magazine.

2 Lock the slide back.

3 Look through the top of the slide, through the entire magazine well. All you should see is the floor or your other hand waving underneath. You should NOT see a magazine or bright, shiny rounds staring back at you. Notice the finger OUTSIDE the trigger guard.

4 Observe the feedramp and chamber of the barrel to ensure that no round is chambered, and double-check by sticking your pinky into the chamber. We know this sounds like we're getting a bit anal, but this is the best method to ensure that your firearm has been properly cleared.

One additional piece of advice—make sure that your fingers are nowhere near the slide release when your pinky is inserted into the chamber, otherwise you'll get a painful lesson on how quickly (and forcefully) the slide will slam closed.

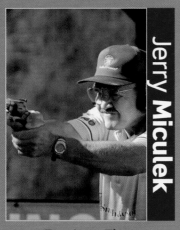

Jerry Miculek

Fourteen Time
International
Revolver Champion

What do you think can be fired faster: a semi-automatic or a revolver? Which one do you think can be reloaded faster? If you guessed a semi-automatic, don't be so sure. Jerry Miculek is a speed shooter and firearms instructor, experienced in nearly every type of firearm made, but revolvers are his first love. He is recognized as the world's fastest revolver shooter, with four world records held, including firing six shots, reloading, and firing six more shots from a revolver in 2.99 seconds. To see this incredible feat, search for Jerry Miculek on YouTube. You won't believe your eyes.

CLEARING REVOLVERS

1 Open the Cylinder.

2 Look through each chamber, and confirm that they are completely clear.

In addition to the four Universal Safety Rules, we've added a few additional topics here:

Safety

1. Educate others on the four Universal Safety Rules, and do not feel bad asking someone to, "watch your muzzle" or to take his finger out of the trigger guard.
2. Prior to handling any firearm, know how to operate it safely. If you're not sure, ask someone who does, but don't assume the guy behind the gun counter is an expert on each and every firearm. Most owner's manuals can also be downloaded from the manufacturer's website.
3. Never depend on safeties in place of the four Universal Safety Rules. Mechanical devices can and do fail! The ultimate "safeties" are your brain and trigger finger.
4. When handing a firearm to someone else, the action should be open.
5. Use only the correct ammunition for your gun, matching up the caliber on the barrel, the ammunition box, and the stamp on the bottom of the cartridge. In addition, prior to using any ammunition with a higher than normal pressure rating (indicated by a +P or +P+ designation) ensure that your firearm is rated for these pressures. A common error is in using .38 Special ammunition with a +P rating in an older .38 Special revolver, not rated for that pressure.
6. Never use drugs (including prescription or over-the-counter drugs) or alcohol prior to or while handling firearms. That's common sense, but doing so may also put you in direct violation of federal and state law.
7. Removing the magazine from a semi-automatic will not remove the round that has been chambered, and most semi-autos will still fire without the magazine in place.
8. Be sure the barrel and action are clear of obstructions including dirt, mud, snow, squib loads, etc. If in doubt, perform the proper clearance procedure, then disassemble your firearm, removing the barrel so that you can perform a visual check.
9. Never shoot at a hard, flat surface; water; or any other object that can cause a shot to ricochet.
10. Store guns and ammunition so they are not accessible to minors (that's federal law) and unauthorized individuals.

Firearm Maintenance

1. Be sure your gun is safe to operate. If you're not sure, bring it to a qualified gunsmith. This is particularly important if you've purchased or inherited a used firearm, or if you notice any cracks, or any change in the firearm's operation (for example, a failure to eject, or a higher frequency of malfunctions).
2. Clean and lubricate your firearm promptly after use. The most common reason for a firearm malfunction is a dirty gun. Plus, these are expensive pieces of equipment. Cleaning your firearm after every use will help to ensure its value is maintained.

On the Range

1. Wear eye and ear protection every time out. If you can't hear instructions on the range, do not crack your ear protection, instead, cup your hand over the back of your ear to indicate that the commands should be repeated.

2. Know and observe all range rules. A key range rule frequently violated is the rule to case and uncase firearms on the firing line, rather than on the shelf or table behind the firing line. This is a major safety violation. In addition, ALWAYS follow the four Universal Safety Rules, and report any individual to the range officer who is not following these rules or who exhibits any unsafe behavior.

3. Never step in front of or behind the firing line.

Holster Safety

1. Ensure that your holster of choice completely covers the trigger and trigger guard. No exceptions.

2. Your holster should retain your firearm in place even if running or jumping. Select a rigid holster that is molded specifically for your firearm rather than a more general "one size fits all" holster.

Otis Cleaning Kit
After the Model 1911, this compact cleaning kit from Otis might just be the greatest invention ever made. From a single kit, nearly every firearm type and caliber can be cleaned, from a .22 caliber handgun, to a 12-gauge shotgun. Properly cleaning and lubricating your firearm after each use will maintain its value, and ensure that it works when you need it.

THE "BELT PARKWAY" CASE

On July 8, 1967, a New York City police detective watched as a bright yellow Camaro crossed several lanes of traffic on the Belt Parkway before crashing into the bushes at the edge of the parkway. Detective Vito DeSerio rushed to the Camaro only to find the driver, 17-year-old Nancy McEwen, slumped over and unresponsive. McEwen was rushed to Coney Island Hospital where the doctors tried desperately to save her life. At 11:15 a.m. McEwen was declared dead. Only then did the doctors discover the cause of her death—hidden by her long blond hair, was a single, bloodless gunshot wound. Returning to the scene, detectives found that all of the Camaro's windows were closed, except for the rear passenger window. Detectives concluded that the shot must have entered that window and could only have come from the sand dunes or reeds of Plum Beach which paralleled the parkway. They immediately set out to search the area for a shell casing, yet none was found. After a ballistics check concluded that the bullet came from an Enfield Model No. 4, the police resorted to a house by house canvass of the neighborhood in an attempt to locate anyone with information about the mystery rifle. In an amazing coincidence, the third stop for the detectives was a Mobile station, where they asked the owner, 46-year-old Theodore DeLisi, whether he owned a rifle. DeLisi answered that he did indeed own a rifle, namely an Enfield Model No. 4. The story that DeLisi told spoke of an amazing series of unlikely timing, incredible ballistics, and a major error in judgment. On the fateful day that Nancy McEwen was shot, DeLisi was heading out to sea for a day of fishing for bluefish. DeLisi brought along his Enfield in case he needed to fend off any sharks that might be attracted by the bluefish bait. Before leaving the inlet, DeLisi decided to test his Enfield on a beer can floating along beside him. His first shot hit the beer can dead center, throwing it across the waves. His second shot missed. Investigators believe that the round ricocheted off the surface of the water, travelling in a ballistic arc no more than 4 feet over the ocean waves, the sand dunes, and the reeds at Plum Beach. Having traveled nearly a mile, the bullet entered the open window of McEwen's moving Camaro, striking her in the head. The lesson? Never forget Universal Rule # 4 (Always be sure of your target and beyond) and never shoot at a hard, flat surface; water; or any other object that can cause a shot to ricochet. Truth *can* be stranger than fiction.

From "Chief" by Albert A. Seedman
and Peter Hellman

SINGLE ACTION (SA) VS. DOUBLE ACTION (DA)

Understanding a handgun's "action" is one of the first steps toward understanding their function and in selecting one that meets your needs. Firearm engineers can argue for hours about the true definition of single action and double action, but functionally, it's a pretty simple concept. Firearms in single action mode will have a shorter, lighter trigger press, and firearms in double action mode will have a longer, heavier trigger press. Mechanically speaking, single action means that the trigger performs a single function, that is, it releases the hammer (which means that the hammer already has to be cocked), while double action means that the trigger press does two things—it first cocks the hammer, then it releases it. Feel free to ignore the mechanical definition and just remember that single action means a shorter and lighter trigger press and double action means a longer and heavier trigger press. Today, some pistols are single action only (SAO), some are double action only (DAO), and some can be fired in either mode like the example shown here, a SIG Sauer P229.

In double action, the distance of the trigger press is approximately ¾ of an inch.

Weight of press is approximately 12 pounds.

In single action, the distance of the trigger press is less than ½ of an inch.

Weight of press is approximately 4 ½ pounds.

The decocked hammer indicates that the firearm is in double action mode. The trigger is set fully forward.

The cocked hammer indicates that the firearm is in single action mode. The trigger is set farther back, closer to the break point.

Decocker
Many semi-automatics with an exposed hammer have a decocker, which allows the hammer to be decocked, placing the firearm in double action mode.

STAINLESS

SIG SAUER

UNDERSTANDING REVOLVERS

Revolvers operate with rounds loaded into a revolving cylinder. Pressing the trigger (in double action mode) or cocking the hammer rotates the cylinder, placing a new round in alignment with the hammer and barrel.

DA/SA Revolvers

Modern revolvers with an exposed hammer are designed to allow the shooter to fire in either single action or double action mode. With the hammer forward (double action mode) a longer, heavier trigger press will rotate the cylinder and cock and release the hammer. Manually cocking the hammer with the thumb puts the gun in single action mode, which might have a trigger press as light as three pounds, and trigger travel as short as 1/16th of an inch. That's nice for accurate target shooting, but is less safe for a self–defense gun. In addition, unlike most DA/SA semi-autos, there is no decocker on revolvers. Decocking a revolver requires very precise control of the hammer and trigger to lower the hammer safely.

Double Action Only (DAO) Revolvers

With its hammer hidden within the frame of the gun, this revolver is double action only (DAO), which provides a consistent trigger press that is longer and heavier than a similar revolver shot in single action mode. This provides an additional level of safety, since a longer, heavier trigger press requires more intent than a short, light trigger press. If you already own a revolver with an exposed hammer, a qualified gunsmith can de-horn the hammer spur.

Front Sight

Muzzle

Barrel
The measured length of the barrel does not include the length of the cylinder.

Cylinder
Cylinders can hold anywhere from five to eight rounds.

Rotation of Cylinder
The teardrop-shaped indents on the side of the cylinder indicate the direction that the cylinder will rotate.

Cylinder Release
Allows the cylinder to be opened for loading and unloading.

Trigger
On double action only (DAO) revolvers, the trigger press will be consistent, usually somewhere between six and ten pounds.

Rear Sight

Hammer

Grips

Revolver grips can be
replaced with aftermarket
grips, allowing the grip
size to be increased
or decreased, and
allowing the
revolver's natural
point of aim (its
"pointability") to
be adjusted for
the individual
shooter.

Trigger

The weight and distance of the trigger
press is much lighter and shorter in single
action mode versus double action—as
light as three pounds in single action,
and as heavy as ten pounds in double
action.

Trigger Guard

UNDERSTANDING SEMI-AUTOMATICS

Semi-autos utilize a moving slide, which slides back using the power of the pistol's recoil (or the blowback of the expanding gases), ejecting the empty casing and re-cocking the hammer or striker. A powerful spring then reverses the direction of the slide, causing it to strip a new round off the top of the magazine, chambering it, and putting the slide back into battery.

Single Action Only

The Model 1911 shown to the right can *only* be fired after the hammer has been cocked, either by racking the slide or with the thumb, which makes it a single action only. The light, short trigger press necessitates that the pistol have a manual safety, which locks the slide and trigger, and allows the gun to be carried "cocked and locked."

DA/SA Semi-Automatic

DA/SA semi-automatics are normally carried with the hammer forward, so the first shot will be a double action shot and all subsequent shots will be in single action (since the moving slide automatically cocks the hammer/striker during the firing cycle). Like most DA/SA semi-automatics, this P229 has a decocker, which allows the hammer to be lowered safely, placing the firearm in double action mode, which is considered to be a safer method for carrying.

Double Action Only (DAO) Semi-Automatic

Like a double action only revolver, DAO semi-automatics have only one firing mode, which will consistently be a longer, heavier trigger press when compared to a similar model shot in single action mode. While this P250 looks similar to the P229, it lacks the exposed hammer, making it double action only (DAO).

Front Sight

Slide

The moving part of the pistol that slides to the rear, ejecting a spent casing and loading a new round.

Slide Lock / Take Down Lever

Most semi-automatics have two separate controls to lock the slide back and to disassemble the firearm (as in the two examples below), while the 1911 combines them into a single control.

Decocker

Rear Sight

Hammer
This Model 1911 can only be fired after the hammer has been cocked, either by racking the slide or with the thumb.

Manual Safety
Thumb-activated safety that locks the slide and trigger.

Grip Safety
Found on Springfield XDs and 1911 models. Unless depressed (as it would be with a normal grip) the trigger is blocked. Most 1911s also have a "beaver tail" that protects the hand from getting bitten by the hammer.

Trigger
On this single action only Model 1911, the trigger press will be light and crisp, typically around four to five pounds.

Grips
The grips on Model 1911s can be swapped for aftermarket grips, but for style and thickness only, not to affect the pistol's natural point of aim.

Magazine Release
Pressing the magazine release will release the magazine from the magazine well. Most semi-automatics have a single magazine release on the left side of the firearm, while others have an ambidextrous release.

Model 1911

In 1906, Colt Manufacturing Co. submitted a Browning-designed semi-automatic pistol to the U.S. Army, which adopted the design on March 29, 1911, giving the pistol the name M1911. World War I increased production to include the Springfield Armory; while World War II ballooned production to include manufacture by Remington Rand, Union Switch & Signal, Ithaca, and even Singer (yes, the sewing machine company). 1911s have served in every military conflict from World War I to the wars in Iraq and Afghanistan, with more than 2.75 million produced for military use. More than 15 manufacturers currently have 1911s in their line-up, and nearly every semi-automatic pistol today can trace its lineage back to Browning's innovative 1911 design.

STRIKER FIRED PISTOLS

The actions described on the previous pages all have one thing in common—the firearms are all hammer operated; that is, regardless of whether or not the hammer is exposed or hidden, it's the hammer that drives the action. Hammer operated firearms fit more neatly into the "single action only, double action only, or DA/SA action" categories than do many popular firearms, including the Glock and Springfield XD(M) shown here. Both Glocks and Springfield XDs are striker fired, and utilize a striker/firing pin held back under the tension of a spring.

Springfield XD "Ultra Safety Assurance" Trigger System

Internally, Springfield XDs are categorized as single action (racking the slide fully cocks the striker/firing pin mechanism), yet externally, they mimic the longer, heavier trigger press of a DAO, similar to the Glock. XD's trigger weights typically fall between 5.5 and 7.7 pounds. While the XD trigger weight and length of press are similar to the Glock, it has a longer trigger reset than a Glock.

Trigger Safety
Found on both the Springfield XD and the Glock, the trigger safety ensures that the gun will only fire when a finger is properly placed on the trigger.

Grip Safety
Found on Springfield XDs and 1911 models. Unless depressed, the trigger is blocked.

Grips

The grips on most composite pistols can't be replaced, but many newer pistols have replaceable backstraps, and ship with several backstraps of various sizes, so that users can tailor the grip size to the size of their hands. Pistols with this feature include the Walther P99, the Smith & Wesson M&P, the Ruger SR9, the HK P30, the new Glock Gen 4 shown here, and the new XD(M) from Springfield on the opposite page.

Glock "Safe Action" Trigger System

Although the BATF has categorized the Glock as a DAO pistol, internally, it falls halfway between a single action and double action. In other words, when the slide is racked, the striker/firing pin mechanism is only *half* cocked. Upon pressing the trigger, the firing pin is fully cocked, then released. Like other striker fired pistols, if a round fails to fire, the Glock does not get a "second strike" capability and the slide must be racked to recock the striker.

WHAT HAPPENS WHEN I PRESS THE TRIGGER?

When the trigger is pressed on a semi-automatic, a bullet leaves the barrel and the slide cycles, ejecting the empty casing and loading a new round, all faster than the eye can see. The step-by-step operations shown here follow the mechanics of a Glock pistol in action.

1 When at "rest," the Glock's firing pin is half-cocked, and the firing pin channel is blocked by the firing pin safety (highlighted). The barrel is "locked" to the slide by the tight fit of the barrel's square chamber, and the slide's square ejection port (visible in the diagram just above the chambered round).

2 When the trigger is pressed, an extension of the trigger bar pushes the firing pin safety up, clearing the firing pin channel. As the trigger continues rearward, the firing pin (highlighted) is fully cocked, then released. The firing pin hits the chambered round's primer with enough force to cause a small explosion, creating a small shower of sparks, which ignite the round's propellant. The solid propellant rapidly turns gaseous, and the expanding gases force the bullet from the casing and accelerate it down the barrel. The barrel's "rifling" (the spiral grooves) causes the bullet to spin, which stabilizes it in flight.

3 At the same time that the bullet is accelerating down the barrel, the handgun is pushed back with an equal amount of force. When the shooter has a solid grip, the momentum of the frame is quickly stopped, but with nothing to stop the slide (and barrel which is still mated to the slide) from its rearward motion, it continues backward, extracting the empty case from the chamber. The small object highlighted in the diagram (called the locking block) unlocks the barrel from the slide, lowering the barrel into position to allow the empty case to hit the ejector, and to allow the new round to be fed into the chamber.

4 The tiny ejector (highlighted) serves one purpose, which is to hit the bottom of the empty case, flipping it to the right through the ejection port.

5 Having traveled as far back as it can go, the slide now reverses direction under pressure from the recoil spring (highlighted). The breech plate pushes against the top-most round, and feeds it into barrel's chamber (also highlighted).

As the slide continues forward, the barrel moves forward with it, pivoting back upward, and locking back into battery. The striker is again half-cocked and the trigger is reset forward.

SAFETY AND DECOCKER VARIETIES

The preceding pages were just a taste of the variations that exist in the marketplace. Just like automobiles, options are endless, including how the firearm's controls operate. Below and to the right are a few additional examples of how controls differ between handguns, including external safeties and decockers. Bottom line? Pick a handgun that works for you and train with it until you can operate its controls in the dark. Someday, you might just have to.

Beretta 92
The Beretta 92 has both a decocker and safety. The hammer is decocked and put on safe by lowering the decocker/safety. Many people carry the Beretta de-cocked but with the safety off, since when decocked, it is in double action mode and is considered safe to carry without the safety engaged. However, see the warning below.

SIG P229
The SIG P229 has a decocker which lowers the hammer by pushing the decocker down. When decocked, the firearm is considered safe to carry and has no additional manual safety.

1911s
The 1911's safety is engaged by pushing it up (the opposite of the Beretta 92). To fire the 1911, the safety is dropped down with a quick action of the thumb. Since the 1911 is a single action only pistol, the hammer must be cocked (either with the thumb, or by racking the slide) before it will fire. For that reason, most people carry the 1911 "cocked and locked" with the hammer back and the safety engaged.

WARNING: MECHANICAL DEVICES CAN FAIL!
The comment that we made earlier in this chapter is worth repeating: NEVER DEPEND ON SAFETIES OR DECOCKING LEVERS! MECHANICAL DEVICES CAN FAIL! Regardless of what safety measures your pistol has, including a manual safety, a grip safety, a trigger safety, or whether it's a double action only with a long, heavy trigger press, the ONLY safety that you should trust is the brain matter between your ears and your trigger finger. If you put your finger in the trigger guard and press the trigger, you should always, always, *always* expect to hear a BANG, and see a hole appear somewhere.

SEMI-AUTO MAGAZINES

While revolvers have a built in device to hold multiple rounds (the cylinder), semi-automatics have rounds fed from a detachable magazine. Magazine types and styles vary, but all can be categorized as single stack or double stack. Single stacks store rounds one on top of the other in a single, straight line, while double stacks store rounds in two staggered rows, allowing more rounds to be stored but resulting in a wider magazine (and larger pistol grip.)

Spring Fatigue?

Some semi-automatic owners are concerned that if they store magazines fully loaded, the internal spring will become fatigued and may fail to properly feed rounds when they are needed. Stop worrying—experts (and engineers) have proven that springs have no "memory" and suffer no additional fatigue when they remain in a compressed state for months or even years. Fatigue *does* occur when the spring is compressed past its design limits or after repeated cycles of compression and release. So *do* replace magazine springs if they've undergone hundreds or thousands of compressions, but *don't* replace them just because you've kept them fully loaded.

Double Stack Magazines

Magazine Lips
The width of the lips is slightly smaller than the diameter of the round, holding the round in place until it's stripped off and loaded into the chamber. When the gap widens on a worn magazine, double-feeds can result.

Follower and Spring
Rounds sit on top of the follower, which is pushed up by the spring. When the last round is fired, the follower pushes up the slide lock on the pistol, thereby locking the slide back.

Base Plate and Base Pad
The base plate secures the spring to the bottom of the magazine, while the pad gives more area when slapping the magazine into the magazine well and also protects the magazine when it hits the floor during a speed reload.

Single Stack Magazines

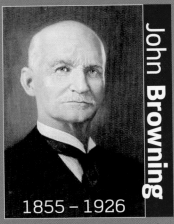

John Browning

1855 – 1926

128 Firearm Patents

John Moses Browning is arguably the most important figure in the development of modern automatic and semi-automatic firearms and is credited with 128 gun patents. Browning received his first patent in 1879 and sold it to Winchester, which released the design as their Model 1885 single shot rifle (still available today from Winchester and Cimarron). Additional Browning designs included the Winchester Model 1887 and Model 1897 shotguns and the lever-action Model 1886, Model 1892, Model 1894 and Model 1895 rifles, most of which are still in production today.

Many shooting aficionados would consider Browning's crowning achievement to be the Model 1911 profiled earlier in this chapter. The author would agree.

WHAT SIZE FIREARM IS RIGHT FOR YOU?

In addition to considering whether you'd like to gravitate toward a revolver or a semi-automatic (plus all of the other features such as the action and additional safety components), you'll also have to consider what size and weight of firearm is right for you, based upon:

» The caliber range that you are comfortable shooting.

» Your size and the way you normally dress.

» Holster options that work for you.

» When and where you plan to carry.

» The weather and time of year.

Trade-Offs

Lighter, smaller firearms usually mean a smaller caliber (and less stopping power) or a more punishing recoil, which might lead to less time on the range. Larger firearms, on the other hand, never get any lighter as the day goes on, which may cause you to leave it at home.

Other Criteria to Consider:

» **Grip size, shape, angle, and material.** Determine how well the grips allow the firearm to properly "point" for you and whether or not your knuckles properly align to the front strap. Grip material and texture are important elements to consider to ensure a solid grip that won't slip. On 1911s, it's worth the extra money to pay for front and backstrap checkering.

» **Grip length:** Short grips are more concealable and "print" less on covering garments, but they provide less space to fit all four fingers of your support hand.

» **Proper placement of your finger on the trigger:** The trigger should rest comfortably in the range between the pad of your finger and first knuckle crease.

» **Balance:** Revolvers and composite framed semi-autos can sometimes feel nose heavy. Always test balance with a fully loaded firearm (make sure this is done on the range, and not on the sales floor).

DEFINING CALIBER AND OTHER MEASUREMENTS

The name of ammunition is typically its caliber (the diameter of the bullet) in either 100ths of an inch or in millimeters, and some other designation such as the company that holds the original patent on the round.

For example, the name .45ACP (Automatic Colt Pistol) tells us that this round is forty-five one-hundreds of an inch in diameter, and that Colt originally patented this round. The round carries the same name regardless of whether it's being shot in a Colt, a Kimber, a Springfield, etc.

Caliber measurements are sometimes inexact; for example, the .38 Special has an actual measurement of 357/1000ths of an inch. That's a holdover from the days of muzzle loading firearms, when the actual diameter of a ball had to be slightly smaller than the barrel in order to allow the ball to fit.

Grains

Grains are a unit of weight, with 7,000 grains per pound, or 437.5 grains per ounce. That means that a 230 grain bullet is just over half an ounce.

Caliber

Caliber is a measurement of the diameter of the bullet (not the casing). The caliber designation has nothing to do with the round's power, it only defines how big of a hole it will make (see example below).

Bullet Weight

The bullet's weight is indicated in grains. There are 7,000 grains in a pound, and handgun bullet weights range from about 40 grains to 230 grains or more.

Case Volume

The relative volume of the case is a good indication of how much propellant the round has. The greater the volume, the more propellant. The more propellant, the faster the bullet will leave the barrel.

Is Caliber all that Matters?

Each of the three rounds to the right are .22 caliber, that is, they'll all make exactly the same size hole in their target. They also happen to all have a 40 grain bullet, yet the differences in case volume (i.e. volume of propellant) makes dramatic differences in the relative velocity of each bullet, translating to dramatic differences in the "power" of each round.

.22 INCH

.22 Long Rifle
Best known as a "plinking" round, the .22 shouldn't be discounted as a self-defense round.

Bullet Weight: 40 Grains

Muzzle Velocity: 1060 FPS

.22 INCH

5.7MM FN
Designed by FN as an alternative to the 9MM, the 5.7MM FN is blazing fast at nearly 2,000 FPS.

Bullet Weight: 40 Grains

Muzzle Velocity: 1950 FPS

.22 INCH

.223 Remington
Best known as the standard NATO round for light rifles, it has a velocity more than triple the .22LR.

Bullet Weight: 40 Grains

Muzzle Velocity: 3330 FPS

KNOCK DOWN POWER

Knock down power is a hot topic of discussion at any gun club—some people will argue for hours that knock down power is directly related to a bullet's kinetic energy, while others will argue that a bigger hole is all that matters. Kinetic energy is measured using the following formula:

Kinetic Energy = $\frac{1}{2} MV^2$

In this formula, M = the mass of the bullet, and V = the speed of the bullet in feet per second. Calculating the mass of a bullet involves converting the weight of the bullet from grains to pounds (there are 7,000 grains in a pound), and needs to figure in gravity (32 feet per second per second). This formula has been the standard for computing a bullet's energy, but it favors velocity over weight, which can result in some oddities. For example, it shows the 9MM bullet having more energy than the .45ACP, which tends to fly in the face of real world military, police, and self–defense statistics. That problem has caused many people to disregard the kinetic energy formula in favor of the Taylor Knockout Factor (TKOF), developed by John Taylor. In addition to using the bullet's velocity and weight, the TKOF formula also includes the bullet's diameter (the size of the hole the bullet will make). Unlike the kinetic energy formula, the TKOF provides *equal* weighting to the bullet's weight, speed, and diameter. The Taylor Knockout Factor is measured using the following formula:

TKOF = (MVD) / 7,000

In this case, M = the weight of the bullet in grains (without calculating in gravity), while V = the speed

of the bullet in feet per second, and D = the diameter of the bullet in inches. The Taylor KO Factor tends to favor heavier, larger caliber bullets when compared to the kinetic energy formula. While either formula provides valuable information, we tend to favor the TKOF measurement (which is how we've placed the rounds to the right), since it seems to better reflect real world statistics.

Feel free to ignore the debate and the formulas— our advice is to simply select the biggest caliber you can shoot well and load it with good self–defense ammunition.

Oh, and for you Dirty Harry fans who might be wondering where the venerable .44 Magnum is on our scale to the right. We'd love to add it, but we'd have to double the height of our book—the .44 Magnum has a TKOF factor of 18.55, nearly double the .357 Magnum.

Self–Defense Caliber Options

We recommend that your self–defense firearm falls within the green or yellow scale to the right (preferably the green), as long these rules apply:

Rule #1: You select a gun that you'll actually carry (that is, it isn't too heavy).

Rule #2: You select the largest caliber that you're comfortable shooting (and comfortable paying for practice ammunition!)

Remember that a .22 caliber in your holster is infinitely more valuable than a .45 left at home.

10MM
Bullet Weight: 200 Grains
Muzzle Velocity: 1200 FPS
Energy: 635 Ft. Lbs.
TKOF: 13.49

.45 ACP
Bullet Weight: 230 Grains
Muzzle Velocity: 835 FPS
Energy: 356 Ft. Lbs.
TKOF: 12.35

.357 Magnum
Bullet Weight: 158 Grains
Muzzle Velocity: 1235 FPS
Energy: 535 Ft. Lbs.
TKOF: 9.95

.40 S&W
Bullet Weight: 180 Grains
Muzzle Velocity: 990 FPS
Energy: 390 Ft. Lbs.
TKOF: 10.18

.357 SIG
Bullet Weight: 125 Grains
Muzzle Velocity: 1350 FPS
Energy: 506 Ft. Lbs.
TKOF: 8.55

.38 Special +P
Bullet Weight: 130 Grains
Muzzle Velocity: 925 FPS
Energy: 247 Ft. Lbs.
TKOF: 6.13

9MM Luger
Bullet Weight: 124 Grains
Muzzle Velocity: 1140 FPS
Energy: 358 Ft. Lbs.
TKOF: 7.14

.380 ACP
Bullet Weight: 95 Grains
Muzzle Velocity: 955 FPS
Energy: 190 Ft. Lbs.
TKOF: 4.93

.38 Special
Bullet Weight: 130 Grains
Muzzle Velocity: 800 FPS
Energy: 185 Ft. Lbs.
TKOF: 5.30

.32 ACP
Bullet Weight: 71 Grains
Muzzle Velocity: 905 FPS
Energy: 129 Ft. Lbs.
TKOF: 2.94

.22 Long Rifle
Bullet Weight: 40 Grains
Muzzle Velocity: 1060 FPS
Energy: 100 Ft. Lbs.
TKOF: 1.33

.25 ACP
Bullet Weight: 50 Grains
Muzzle Velocity: 760 FPS
Energy: 64 Ft. Lbs.
TKOF: 1.36

Rounds shown in actual size

TAYLOR KNOCKOUT FACTOR

15
14
13
12
11
10
9
8
7
6
5
4
3
2
1
0

WHY USE HOLLOWPOINTS FOR SELF-DEFENSE?

In 1998, the New York City Police Department became the last major police department in the United States to switch from full metal jacket ammunition to hollowpoints. Police Commissioner Howard Safir commented, "We are going to switch to hollowpoint ammunition as soon as we receive it. They are much safer than fully jacketed bullets, which will go through a person and then continue on and hit innocent victims." Commissioner Safir didn't make this statement in a vacuum. A report that year by the New York Times confirmed that in a two–year period, 46% of innocent bystanders that were struck by police bullets were hit by rounds that passed through an attacker's body, or through another object. Equally troubling, 39% of police officers struck by "friendly fire" were hit by bullets that overpenetrated the bodies of attackers the police were battling. Advocates for the switch included the Civilian Complaint Review Board, the independent agency charged with monitoring the police. In addition to the reduced chance of overpenetration, advocates of the change also observed that hollowpoints had a greater chance of stopping an attacker with fewer bullets, also lessening the chance that innocent bystanders might be injured. Today, nearly every police department in the United States issues hollowpoint ammunition as standard issue. While you'll need to make an individual decision as to whether or not hollowpoint ammunition is the right choice for you, your decision might be made a bit easier by contacting your local police department and asking them what *they* carry. Note that hollowpoint ammunition is *not* legal in all states.

》Hollowpoints operate on hydraulics—that is, the fluid contained within a body provides adequate pressure within the hollowpoint's cavity to rapidly expand the cavity, and fold back the lead core and pre-scored copper jacket. While this is occurring, the increased diameter causes a rapid deceleration of the bullet, eventually slowing and stopping it. This deceleration occurs much more rapidly in a hollowpoint bullet that has fully expanded, when compared to a bullet that is not designed to expand (such as a full metal jacket), or a hollowpoint that fails to expand because of a lack of velocity, or one that has become clogged with heavy clothing, which can cause the hydraulic process to fail.

SELF-DEFENSE AMMUNITION OPTIONS

There are too many self-defense rounds for us to comment on, but we've described a few of the most popular below. You'll notice that we've focused on "traditional" hollowpoints (the EFMJ aside), rather than more exotic rounds such as frangibles, which are designed to shatter on impact to avoid overpenetration.

ROUND	DESCRIPTION	CHARACTERISTICS
Hornady TAP FPD (For Personal Defense)	Uses "low flash" powder to protect night vision. Also has black nickel plating to provide better feeding and eliminate corrosion.	Both the low flash characteristics and nickel coating make this a great home defense round. The black case color is also pretty cool, and actually feels slick to the touch.
Federal Hydra-Shok	Copper Jacketed Hollowpoint, with unique center post to provide controlled expansion.	Until recently, the Hydra-Shok was almost universally adopted as the ammunition of choice for police departments across the U.S. Federal recently released an update to the Hydra-Shok, called the HST, which seems to offer more consistent expansion than its predecessor and is quickly replacing the Hydra-Shok as the ammunition of choice for law enforcement.
Federal EFMJ (Expanding Full Metal Jacket)	Looks like a full metal jacket, but has a scored copper jacket covering an internal rubber nose and lead core.	The full metal jacket look and characteristics allow this round to feed much more reliably than traditional hollowpoints, yet the expansion is still impressive. We've personally tested the expansion of a .45 ACP that mushroomed to .70. Unlike traditional hollowpoints which rely on hydraulics to expand, the EFMJ operates on deceleration, with the scored jacket collapsing over the rubber nose upon impact, resulting in a pancaked bullet.
Magtech First Defense & Cor-Bon DPX	Solid Copper Hollowpoint, resulting in 100% weight retention.	The Magtech First Defense and Cor-Bon DPX rounds are 100% copper, without any jacket that can tear away. This results in 100% weight retention, which means that 100% of the bullet penetrates to the full depth.
Speer Gold Dot	Copper Jacketed Hollowpoint with a wider and deeper cavity than traditional hollowpoints.	With so many "shall issue" states, firearm manufacturers have been selling more short barrel pistols than ever before. Those short barrels result in lower muzzle velocities, which can result in hollowpoints failing to open. The Gold Dot line has much larger and deeper hollowpoint cavities, resulting in positive expansion, even with short barrel handguns.

WHY DOES BARREL LENGTH MATTER?

Why does barrel length matter? A longer barrel will result in a higher velocity bullet, since there is more time for the bullet to accelerate before the gases dissipate. For the same model pistol with different barrel lengths (for example, Springfield XDs with 3", 4" and 5" barrels) velocity can vary by as much as 300 feet per second for the same weight bullet.

So why does that matter? When it comes to punching holes through paper, it really doesn't matter. When it comes to using a firearm for self–defense, it *does* matter. A higher velocity round is more likely to stop a violent attacker because of deeper penetration of the bullet and a higher probability that hollowpoint bullets will expand. There used to be a "magic number" of about 1,000 feet per second before a hollowpoint bullet would expand, but with newer hollowpoint bullets with larger cavities, that barrier is no longer critical.

Feet Per Second

Sample Muzzle Velocities by Barrel Length

CALIBER	5 INCHES	4 INCHES	3 INCHES	2 INCHES
.38 Special	1062	1014	878	733
9MM Luger	1233	1173	1105	1019
.40 S&W	1193	1136	1071	985
.45 ACP	1047	1003	911	857

Source: ballisticsbytheinch.com

AMMUNITION CARE AND STORAGE

Taking care of your ammunition (including storing it safely) is as important as caring for your firearm. Here's what you should remember:

» Keep ammunition in a cool, dry area and store it separately from your firearm.

» Keep ammunition in its original factory box or carton.

» Do not expose ammunition to water or any gun solvents or oils. They can leak into the seam between the bullet and the casing, allowing the propellant to become damp and unreliable, possibly leading to a hang fire.

» As mentioned in our "Additional Safety Considerations" section, use only the correct ammunition for your gun, matching up the caliber on the barrel, the ammunition box, and the stamp on the bottom of the cartridge. In addition, prior to using any ammunition with a higher than normal pressure rating (indicated by a +P or +P+ designation), ensure that your firearm is rated for these pressures.

» Inspect ammunition prior to loading. Discard rounds with damaged cases, corrosion, or loose bullets.

» Avoid chambering and un-chambering the same round multiple times, which can lead to projectile set-back. Put simply, projectile set-back is when the bullet becomes jammed back farther into the case than it is meant to be, which can increase the pressure of the round, resulting in a damaged firearm (and damaged hands, eyes, etc.) This typically occurs when someone clears a firearm every night before storing it (dropping the magazine and ejecting the chambered round) then reinserting the ejected round on top of the magazine.

» Replace personal protection ammunition at least once a year (ammunition that has been loaded into your firearm, but not fired). That's not because the ammunition goes bad (we've fired .38 Specials that were found in the in-law's basement and were at least 40 years old). It's because repeated heating and cooling of your firearm and ammunition can lead to condensation, which can lead to corrosion of both.

» Understand that not all types of ammunition will feed reliably in your firearm. In particular, for self–defense ammunition, you should practice with at least 200 to 250 rounds before selecting your personal protection ammunition of choice.

Myth BUSTED: The Story about the .22 "Fuse"

Much to the dismay of story tellers everywhere, the urban myth about a .22 used as a car fuse was busted on one of our favorite shows, "Myth Busters." As told, the story has two friends returning home from a night out hunting frogs, when their car blew a fuse. Lacking a spare, they inserted a .22 long rifle cartridge in its place, which eventually "cooked off," shooting the driver and seriously injuring him. Myth Busters concluded that while it was possible for a round to cook off if a serious short occurred, it was unlikely to seriously injure or kill someone. During each test, the high-speed video showed the bullet and casing simply blowing apart in opposite directions with the lighter case flying away with more velocity than the heavier bullet. It was apparent that without a breech plate to rest against or a barrel to accelerate down, a cooked off round would be more likely to give a "nasty bruise" than to prove lethal.

The Death of Brandon Lee

Squib loads are known more for blown barrels than fatalities, but that's exactly what happened to Brandon Lee on the set of his movie "The Crow." On March 31, 1993, Lee was killed while filming a scene in which his character was, ironically, shot and killed. The series of fatal errors began much earlier, when the film crew created their own "dummy" rounds by using real cartridges. The crew attempted to make the live rounds inert by removing the bullets and dumping out the propellant before reinserting the bullets, but they failed to remove the live primers. At some point in the filming, the trigger was pressed and a squib load occurred, lodging a bullet in the barrel. During the fateful scene, the same revolver was loaded with blanks, and fired at Lee. The resulting propellant charge was enough to drive the lodged bullet from the barrel into Lee's torso, resulting in his death.

COMMON AMMUNITION MALFUNCTIONS

No "Pop" from the primer, no "Bang" from the shockwave, just the "Click" of the hammer falling.

Just the "Pop" of the primer, but no "Bang" for up to a minute. Very rare.

Just the "Pop" of the primer and low or no recoil. PUT IT DOWN!

Misfire

Occurs when the primer fails to ignite after being struck by the firing pin. This causes a "Type One" failure and must be cleared with the procedure on the following page. The usual suspect? A dirty firearm, rather than a bad round.

Hang Fire

A delay in the firing of the round after the primer has been struck by the firing pin. Typically caused when moisture or oil has found its way inside the cartridge, which can cause any dry propellant to act like a fuse. If that fuse burns its way to a concentration of dry propellant, the round can fire up to a full minute after the trigger was pressed.

Squib Load

Often caused by a round that has no propellant—the primer's small explosion is enough to drive the bullet from the casing, but not enough to make it all the way down the barrel. If you believe you've had a squib load, stop firing immediately, or you risk a damaged barrel, damaged hand, damaged eyes, etc.

SEMI-AUTO MALFUNCTIONS

Semi-autos can have failures for a variety of reasons:

1. A round has misfired and remains chambered, referred to as a **"Type One" Malfunction**.

2. The ejected casing has failed to completely eject and is caught between the slide and the barrel, known as a "stovepipe" or a **"Type Two" Malfunction**.

3. The lack of a solid grip allows the entire gun to shift rearward, resulting in the slide's failure to separate from the frame far enough to eject the empty casing, and the empty casing is reloaded in the chamber.

Clearing Type One & Type Two Malfunctions

Type One and Type Two malfunctions are cleared with a three step process:

1 **SLAP** the bottom of the magazine to fully seat it.

2 **RACK** the slide fully to the rear. Notice that we're grasping the slide between the palm of the hand and all four fingers, rather than pinching the rear of the slide between the thumb and index finger which is referred to as "sling shotting."

3 **ROLL** the gun to the right to dump out the bad round / empty case. Releasing the slide (not easing it forward) loads a new round.

If you've completed the three malfunction clearance steps on the previous page and discover that the slide isn't going forward, you most likely have a **"Type Three" malfunction** which include failures to feed and failures to eject. These malfunctions are usually caused by one of two culprits:

1. A worn extractor, which can leave the empty case in the chamber of the gun after the slide cycles.

2. A bad magazine, which can cause two rounds to be fed at the same time.

Either failure will try to force two objects into the chamber at the same time, in effect, locking the slide in place and disabling the firearm.

Clearing Type Three Malfunctions

Type Three malfunctions are cleared with these additional steps:

4 **LOCK** the slide to the rear.

5 **DROP** the magazine (it may be necessary to pry it from the gun if a double-feed has it locked in place). Once the magazine is dropped, more often than not, you'll see two rounds hit the floor.

6 **RACK** the slide three times to remove any additional obstructions.

7 **REINSERT** the magazine (or insert a spare, since the magazine itself might be causing the problem) and rack the slide to chamber a new round.

HOME DEFENSE SHOTGUN FUNDAMENTALS

Conventional wisdom is that a shotgun is the best firearm for home defense when compared to a pistol, but that "wisdom" is usually based upon the incorrect theory that you can't miss with a shotgun since they create a "pattern" of shot, rather than a single hole. At 20 to 30 yards that matters, but at seven feet, a shotgun pattern will typically be no larger than a baseball, and at 21 feet, it will typically be no larger than a basketball. That means that shotguns still require deliberate aiming, and that shooting from the hip or selecting a shotgun with just a pistol grip and no buttstock might result in a missed shot. Where shotguns *do* give us an edge is in the load that they deliver.

to a ghost ring or consider a TruGlo™ front sight; and many tactical shotguns can also be mounted with red dot scopes for easier point shooting, giving you the ability to look at your attacker, not the front sight. Surefire also offers mounted lights via replacement forends for Remington, Benelli, Mossberg, and Winchester models, which provide both a pressure sensitive pad for momentary activation, or a constant on/off switch. Options for home defense shotguns range from your granddaddy's old side-by-side, to autoloaders like the Benelli M4 shown here.

At close quarters, even #6 or #7 shot loads will stop or disable an attacker, and 00 or 000 buckshot will fire the near equivalent of six to eight .380 pistol rounds, all delivered within that baseball sized pattern. Shotguns, like any long gun, also give us a much longer sight radius (the distance between the rear sight and the front sight), aiding in accuracy. If upgrading an existing shotgun for a home defense gun, we recommend that you upgrade the sights

Reliability counts more than the action you choose, but any multi-shell shotgun has advantages over single- or double-barrels. If buying new, we recommend a 12 gauge with an 18-inch barrel and ghost ring sights or a red dot scope. On the following page, we've recommended two low recoil buckshot loads which are appropriate if you have at least two to three layers of drywall between yourself (the defender) and any loved ones or neighbors. Otherwise, we'd recommend backing up to a #4 load or smaller. Steer clear of magnum loads—you're delivering those pellets tens of feet, not hundreds.

THE AR-15 PLATFORM

A favorite punching bag of the anti-gun movement, the semi-automatic AR-15 rifle is often referred to by the popular media as an "assault rifle" or a "machine gun." The AR-15 is neither of those things. While the AR-15 is tailored after the light rifle carried by American soldiers and Marines (the M16), that doesn't mean that the AR-15 is a machine gun (we should also note that the M16 isn't even a machine gun, since it's only capable of firing three-round bursts, rather than full automatic fire). Additionally, the fact that the AR-15 stock is made from black plastic and composite materials, doesn't mean that it's any more powerful than the average hunting rifle with a wooden stock. In fact, the AR-15, chambered in the Remington .223, is considered too *light* a caliber to be legal in many states for deer hunting, with less than half of the kinetic energy as the .30-06 (pronounced "thirty-ought-six"), the most common deer hunting round on the market. The attractiveness of the AR-15 for someone considering a firearm for home defense (or just for plinking), is the same thing that continues to attract the U.S. military to the M16 more than forty years after it was first adopted as its standard light rifle, and that's the rifle's utter reliability; its low recoil and light weight; and its almost unlimited ability to be customized with hundreds of accessories. However, as reliable and ubiquitous as the AR-15 is considered today, it wasn't always that way.

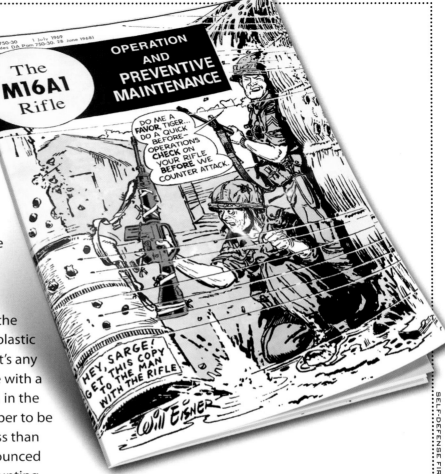

A Short History of the AR-15

The brainchild of Eugene Stoner, chief engineer at the Armalite Division of Fairchild Engine and Airplane Corporation, the AR-15 (AR stands for "Armalite Rifle"), was conceived as a short range, light-weight replacement to the M14 (the U.S. Military's standard battle rifle from 1959 to 1970), after statistics from World War II and the Korean War confirmed that most combat occurred at far less than 100 yards, and that the heavy M14, weighing in at 12.75 pounds and firing the powerful .308 round, could prove unwieldy for the average infantryman. Although the U.S. Army first tested the AR-15 during a set of trials in 1959, it was actually the U.S. Air Force that first adopted the rifle in 1962 with an initial order of 8,500 rifles, designating the new rifle the M16. During their tests, the Air Force found that 43 percent of testers were able to qualify as "experts" with the AR-15, while only 22 percent of testers on the M14 were able to do so. They also found that the AR-15 had a failure rate of just 2.5 rounds per 1,000 rounds fired, compared to the M14, which experienced a failure rate of 16 per 1,000. U.S. Special Forces operating in Vietnam soon followed suit, ordering 85,000 by 1963, with more than 1,000 destined for the South Vietnamese Army. In 1963, Secretary of Defense Robert McNamara suspended production of the M14 rifle, and in 1966, concluded that the AR-15/M16 was to be the new, standard issue rifle for the U.S. Military.

Reliability Problems in Vietnam

While the Air Force trials in 1960 showed a failure rate of just 2.5 per 1,000 rounds fired, a series of small errors led to a much larger failure rate in the harsh conditions of Vietnam. Chief among the errors was the military's failure to provide adequate cleaning kits with the rifles, and a failure to provide adequate training on how to keep the rifles clean. By 1967 that error was corrected, and new rifles began to be shipped with more complete cleaning kits. In a nod to the average age of U.S. Soldiers and

Marines in Vietnam, the military even went as far as commissioning Mad Magazine artist Will Eisner to create a comic book, explaining exactly how to properly maintain the M16 rifle in the field.

The Modern AR-15

While the early failures in Vietnam stuck with the AR-15's reputation for the next two decades, today, AR-15s are widely considered to be one of the most reliable platforms on the market. While AR-15s can be bought off-the-shelf fully configured, most aficionados prefer to order the upper, lower, and accessories separately, so that the rifle can be tailored specifically to the purchaser's needs. In that way, the AR-15 is really the "erector set" of firearm platforms, with literally thousands of variations available from the base platforms. If you'd like to take the DIY approach, it's important to know that the AR-15's "lower" (the portion of the firearm containing the trigger control group) is what's actually considered the firearm, so you'll need to make that purchase through a licensed dealer. All other components can be picked up off the shelf to create an AR-15 all your own.

>> Since the early days of the Vietnam War, the M16 has seen service in every military conflict including Iraq and Afghanistan. The M16's semi-automatic counterpart, the AR-15, is a trusted tool of police departments and responsibly armed citizens across the country.

Rail System

Most off the shelf AR-15s will come with the same type of plastic stocks seen since Vietnam, but replacing those with a rail system as seen here, allows any number of accessories to be attached, such as the pistol grip or red dot scope also shown here. Lights, lasers, etc., will also mount securely to this standardized rail system.

Folding Front Sight

This folding front sight allows the sight to be dropped out of the way when using a red dot scope, yet quickly raised if the battery in the scope fails. If installed correctly, the front and rear sight should line up exactly in the center of the scope, allowing what's referred to as "co-witnessing" of both sight systems.

Flash Suppressor or Compensator

Fixed to the end of the barrel, flash suppressors are intended to reduce the size of the "flash" that can occur as burning propellent leaves the barrel. That flash can be particularly irritating when firing in low light, since it can disrupt your night vision. Compensators look similar to suppressors, although rather than having horizontal channel cuts, they'll typically have angled holes, which will direct the dissipating gases in a direction opposite the rifle's natural muzzle rise.

Forward Pistol Grip

While the AR-15 can be fired like a traditional hunting rifle by placing the support hand under the forestock, that position can be a bit awkward if firing for an extended period of time at the range. A forward pistol grip, or the Angled Fore Grip from Magpul, can provide a more natural way of holding the rifle. Surefire also offers a number of pistol grip / tactical light combinations, which allows the operator to hold the rifle steady, and momentarily light up a scene by squeezing pressure pads integrated into the vertical grip.

Magazine

AR-15 magazines are traditionally made from steel, but plastic magazines like this one from Magpul are gaining in popularity. Personally, we're huge Magpul fans.

Red Dot Scope

This red dot scope from Aimpoint is a non-magnifying scope, which provides a holographic red dot which appears to float in the middle of the scope. This allows the shooter to focus on the target with both eyes open, and simply place the red dot on target before pressing the trigger.

Folding Rear Sight

This folding front sight allows the sight to be dropped out of the way when using a red dot scope, yet quickly raised if the battery in the scope fails.

Charging Handle

Pulling the charging handle to the rear, retracts the bolt. Pressing the bolt lock when the charging handle is fully to the rear will lock the bolt back.

Selector Switch

As a semi-automatic, the AR-15 has only two settings on the selector switch: safe and semi. Rotating the switch to "semi" and pressing the trigger will fire one round for each trigger press.

Collapsible Stock

Unlike a fixed stock, collapsible stocks allow the user to tailor the length of stock for their specific height, neck length, etc. Most shooters will collapse the stock much shorter than a stock length they'd use on a traditional hunting rifle—the shorter length allows them to take up more of an isosceles stance (with both shoulders squared to the target), rather than a traditional rifle stance, which would angle the shooting shoulder to the rear.

Bolt Lock and Bolt Release

When the charging handle is pulled back (pulling the bolt back with it), pushing on the bottom of the bolt lock will lock the bolt to the rear. Pressing on the top of the bolt release will allow the bolt to travel forward.

Pistol Grip

Like it sounds, the AR-15 pistol grip allows the shooter to take up a grip reminiscent of shooting a pistol, rather than a traditional rifle grip, which forces the hand back at an odd angle. Like all AR-15 accessories, pistol grips can be purchased in all shapes and sizes, including this example molded for the fingers.

OTHER USE OF FORCE OPTIONS

As part of our personal protection plans, we may want to consider other "use of force" options which have a lesser chance of killing an attacker, and a lesser chance of putting us in legal peril, such Tasers, pepper spray, knives, and impact weapons. When considering these other options, it's important to remember that while a firearm can have a disabling or deterrent effect out to dozens of feet, these other devices will require you to be within 10—15 feet of the attacker for a Taser or pepper spray, and within arm's reach for an edged or impact weapon.

How Do Tasers Work?

More properly called an electronic control device (Taser® is a brand name), these devices are designed to send a high-voltage, low-amperage electrical charge through the body of an attacker. The charge confuses the body's own natural electrical signals, incapacitating the attacker. Consumer models, such as the Taser C2, utilize cartridges that when fired, release compressed air to shoot two probes connected to wires in the direction of the attacker (up to 15 feet), which then embed themselves in the attacker's clothes or skin. The device is designed to deliver a 30 second shock, allowing the victim to drop the Taser, and retreat to cover. Detractors have claimed that criminals will use Tasers to incapacitate their victims, however, Taser has developed an innovative device within the C2, which showers the ground with 20 to 30 "confetti like" tags, containing an identification number that can be traced by police. Taser also requires that purchasers pass a background check prior to device activation.

» The C2 comes in a small package with replaceable cartridges. Options include a built-in laser and LED light to assist in aiming. If the user misses an attacker with the ejected probes, the device can also be used in a direct contact mode, using built-in contacts on the face of the device. Taser has a lifetime guarantee and will replace the device for free if it is used in a defensive situation.

TASER® C2

» When fired, the C2 releases compressed air to shoot two probes connected to wires in the direction of the attacker (up to 15 feet), which then embed themselves in the attacker's clothes or skin. The device is designed to deliver a 30-second shock, allowing the victim to drop the Taser, and retreat to cover. To avoid misuse, the C2 showers the ground with 20 to 30 "confetti like" tags, containing an identification number that can be traced by police.

TASER® C2

Pepper Spray

The active ingredient in pepper spray is oleoresin capsicum (OC), a chemical found in cayenne peppers (hence the name "pepper" spray). OC affects mucous membranes like the eyes, nose, throat, and lungs, and causes instant capillary dilation, causing the eyelids to shut. The bronchial tubes may also swell tightly, making it hard for the attacker to breathe. Sprayed into an attacker's face, pepper spray may incapacitate an attacker for as long as 45 minutes. Pepper spray potency can be measured in a variety of ways, including showing the percentage of OC contained in the spray (although this makes no statement about the potency of the OC itself); or "heat" can be measured in Scoville Heat Units (SCU) which is a subjective measurement of the dilution required before no heat is detectable (although some manufacturers will show the SCU of the base OC, while others will show the SCU of the diluted OC); or potency can be expressed in CRCs (Capsaicin and related Capsaicinoids) which measures the actual percentage of heat and pain producing active ingredients. Our advice is to take a look at all three numbers, but use the CRC rating as the final determining factor when picking out a pepper spray that works for you. As a quick litmus test, the U.S. Government requires a CRC rating of at least one-percent for bear deterrent pepper spray.

Kimber Pepperblaster
The PepperBlaster from Kimber, stores OC and benzyl alcohol in separate tubes, which are mixed when the trigger is depressed. The PepperBlaster delivers its spray at 90 miles an hour. The Pepperblaster has a CRC rating of 2.4%.

CHAPTER 3

SHOOTING FUNDAMENTALS

» Muscle Memory Explained
» Proper Grip
» Stance or "Shooting Platform"
» Point Shooting
» Flash Sight Picture
» Sighted Fire
» Trigger Control

As much as we enjoy plinking at the range, the goal of this chapter is to introduce you to the shooting fundamentals required for self–defense. As you'll read in our physiological section in Chapter Five, when we're under the extreme stress of a violent attack, our higher brain will very likely check out, and to one degree or another, automated responses will take over. Because of that, if we have a choice between a complex method of doing things and a simple method, we're going to have to pick simple. If we have a choice between a method that embraces those automated responses or fights them, we need to pick the method that embraces them. As you'll see in this chapter, we're going to look at the shooting fundamentals as a set of building blocks—if we can master one skill, the next skill becomes easier to accomplish. On the other hand, if we blow one of the skills, it will affect the rest. Mastering these fundamentals won't qualify you for the U.S. Shooting team or win you the Bianchi Cup, but they *will* provide the proper building blocks to work toward defensive accuracy, which we'll further define in this chapter.

Our goal when practicing these skills should be consistency, which allows us to effectively bake the fundamentals into the neural pathways of our brain (creating what most people would call "muscle memory"), which we'll explain further in this chapter. Whatever skill or task isn't previously hardwired into those pathways, is probably not a task that we'll be able to accomplish during a violent attack. They say that "practice makes perfect," but that's not quite true. Practice makes *permanent*, so for every evolution of these fundamentals that you conduct on the range, take the time to make them, well, perfect. The great news is that there are just four building blocks to master, including grip, stance (or "shooting platform"), target alignment, and trigger control.

We're going to start with what we consider to be the basis of all other shooting fundamentals, namely, taking up a proper shooting grip. This section not only explains why we think a proper grip is so important, it also provides a number of illustrations showing exactly how to get your grip right.

In our section on shooting platforms, we'll introduce you to the shooting stance that was a staple of nearly every police academy for nearly four decades, but we'll go on to explain why most police academies *and* civilian training courses have moved beyond the Weaver stance, and are now teaching what Rob Pincus would describe as a "natural and neutral" shooting platform, designed to match the body's and the mind's automated responses to the extreme stress that will accompany any violent attack.

Our topic on target alignment will discuss the balance of speed versus accuracy, and what are options might be when moving from one end of the scale to the other. Those topics will include using unsighted fire or "point" shooting, using a flash sight picture, and using precise sight alignment, which are the three major options when it comes to aligning our barrel to the target. We'll also discuss when one option might be preferable over the other, but we'll also discuss why the automated responses that we'll very likely experience might just choose the method for us. We'll wrap up this chapter with a topic on trigger control where we'll explain how you can train yourself to press the trigger without disrupting target alignment, and how you can learn about your trigger's reset point.

WHAT EXACTLY IS "MUSCLE MEMORY?"

We've all tossed out the phrase "muscle memory" when talking about learning a repetitive skill, regardless of whether that "skill" is playing golf, playing the piano, or drawing from the holster. Unfortunately, muscles themselves have no "memory," so, where exactly are these repetitive skills being stored? The answer is the cerebellum, which is the brain's memory center. When a certain skill or movement is practiced repeatedly, pathways are actually modified in the cerebellum to store and link individual movements, similar to how individual still frames are stored and linked on a spool of film. The more the skill or movement is repeated, the stronger the pathways linking the individual steps. The result can be near automatic playback of the stored memory of movements. As an example, new students learning to draw from the holster will learn that there are four steps involved, and they'll practice those movements in four distinct steps. But after thousands of repetitions, those four movements will have become fluid, and the "experts" may not even be able to answer the question, "How many steps does it take to draw the handgun from the holster?" To them, the process is fluid and automatic (they might even say, "It takes just one step.") No one knows just how many times a task or series of tasks will need to be repeated before it's ready for "automatic playback," but suffice to say, it's going to be more than plinking at the range a couple times a year. Dry firing, drawing from the holster with a cleared firearm, and virtual simulations are all ways that these pathways can be built, all without a shot being fired.

Making Pathways Permanent

The basic and advanced drills that we'll discuss in Chapter Seven all have one thing in common—they're all fundamentally rooted in the building blocks discussed in this chapter. Regardless of how fast you might draw from the holster, if you haven't mastered trigger control, all you'll end up with is a very fast miss, and that won't impress anyone, especially a bad guy. If you've mastered unsighted fire, but you haven't put in thousands of repetitions disengaging your gun's safety, you might find yourself with an inoperable gun when it counts, because the situation didn't give you time to *think*, it only gave you time to *act*.

When can you Quit Practicing the Fundamentals?

That begs the question, "When can you quit practicing the fundamentals, and just focus on the advanced stuff?" The short answer is, never. One of our good friends who happens to be a retired Navy SEAL, once took the time to estimate how many rounds he'd fired in his Navy career—his conservative estimate was somewhere above one-and-a-half *million* rounds. Yet if you asked him how he started each range drill to this day, he'd tell you that he always starts with dry firing (explained in Chapter Seven), and a number of basic drills to reinforce the fundamentals, before he moved on to more complex exercises. Regardless of whether his training exercise for the day was rappelling from a helicopter into a fortified compound, or landing a zodiac onto an oil platform, he'd start and end the day with dry firing, and a review of the fundamentals. If that's good enough for the Navy SEALS, it's good enough for us.

Whether you're learning to draw from the holster or learning the Macarena (you know who you are), repetition of any task begins to build new pathways into the cerebellum, connecting individual movements into a continuous series of movements for near automatic "playback." Similar to how a film projector can take individual still frames and make them appear as though they flow together into continuous movement, the cerebellum can do the same thing with these repetitive tasks. The key here is that you'll need to practice them until they *become* repetitive.

PROPER GRIP

Although all of the shooting fundamentals we'll cover in this chapter are important, we're going to start with what we consider to be the fundamental of all shooting fundamentals, namely, learning how to take up a proper grip when using a handgun. If you've never had formal handgun instruction, it may sound a little basic to discuss the proper way to "grip" a handgun—in other words, don't you just pick it up, point it down range, and start pressing the trigger? Well, in a way, it isn't any more complicated than that, but before stepping into *how* to take up a proper grip, it's probably a fair place to start by talking about what the *goal* of a proper grip is. If your answer is to hold the handgun, you'd only be half correct.

When setting up your grip, the pistol should be placed firmly into your firing hand like you are making a fist, with the web of your hand high and centered on the back strap. The firing hand thumb should be high, to create a space for the support hand.

The trigger finger is OUTSIDE THE TRIGGER GUARD and is pressed on the frame or slide, and the middle finger is bumped up against the bottom of the trigger guard.

The ultimate goal of a proper grip is creating and maintaining *control* of your handgun during the firing cycle. Other instructors might take issue with our choice of grip as the most important fundamental over other shooting fundamentals. That's a debate we recently had with a fellow instructor, who argued that precise trigger control had to be more important than grip. To demonstrate this, he had a number of us stand on the firing line and fire one round at a target at 50 feet while daintily holding our pistol with our thumb and middle finger, and slowly pressing the trigger, all while maintaining perfect sight alignment. Of course, most of us hit fairly close to our point of aim. His point was that if you could make an accurate shot at that distance with almost no grip pressure at all,

Wrap the fingers of your support hand firmly around the firing hand with the index finger pressed firmly against the bottom of the trigger guard and the meaty part of your support hand nestled into the open space on the grip left by the firing hand. To create the perfect "seal" between both hands, the thumbs are stacked, with the third knuckle of the support hand nestled in the space between the first and second knuckle of the firing hand. No part of the firearm grip should be visible between your fingers, or between the strong hand and support hand.

Solid isometric pressure should be applied from the front and the rear (described as a "push-pull" action, with the shooting hand pushing forward, and the support hand pulling back), which will aid in recoil management. The majority of pressure holding the firearm in place should come from the isometric tension between the two hands, rather than from trying to hold the pistol in place by finger pressure alone. That allows your trigger finger to work independently of the other fingers on your shooting hand, avoiding what's referred to as "milking" the trigger.

then trigger control *must* be more important than grip. While it was a cute trick to show at the range, taking four or five seconds to fire one round at a stationary target 50 feet away, had about as much to do with an actual critical incident as Wii Sports Resort has to do with competing in the Ironman Triathlon. Here's why. As our friend Rob Pincus would point out, critical incidents are usually *fast*, they're usually *close* (with nearly ninety percent falling between 9—15 feet), and when rounds are fired, *multiple* rounds are usually fired—in other words, the mythical one shot stop was usually just that, a myth. So much for one round fired at 50 feet having any meaning. If multiple rounds might be necessary to stop a bad guy from stabbing you, beating you, choking you, or raping you, then it stands to reason that the faster you can put those rounds on target, the sooner the stabbing, beating, choking, or raping will stop. Two things are going to affect your ability to deliver rounds quickly— first, how quickly you can bring your firearm back on target after the muzzle flips during recoil; and second, how quickly you can cycle the trigger. To quote Pincus, "Anyone can hit with a sloppy grip if they use the sights, but a solid grip is required to shoot intuitively, and to get faster follow-up shots."

As seen from above, the tip of the trigger finger, when placed on the slide, should be directly across from the tip of the thumb on the support hand. Most new shooters will find their support thumb being much farther back than the tip of the tip of the trigger finger—this is corrected by rotating the support hand farther forward, resulting in what's referred to as a "thumbs forward" grip.

That's not just a theory of Rob's, it also finds its way into competitive shooting. While comparing choreographed competition to an actual critical incident can only go so far, this comparison might be worth it. When asked how they're able to deliver so many rounds on target so quickly, many competitors will explain that a good solid grip and full arm extension allows them to press the trigger as fast as they are physically able, in fact, they'll often refer to that technique as "slapping" or "mashing" the trigger (which is not exactly the kind of trigger control that our colleague had in mind). If we bring that theory back to how it might apply to surviving a critical incident, a solid grip means more rounds on target in a shorter amount of time. Any sloppiness in your grip means a lack of control during recoil, a higher muzzle flip, and slower follow-up shots. Think about it this way. Instead of the range exercise that our colleague used in an attempt to prove that trigger control was more important than grip, let's try a new exercise, but this one with a different set of rules. Instead of firing one round at a target 50 feet away, let's place the target at 12 feet (right in the heart of where most defensive shootings occur), and fire as many rounds as we can into the target's center of mass in three seconds. Using our colleague's technique, you'd be lucky to place more than one round on target, as you fought to bring the handgun back under control after the first round was fired. On the other hand, if you fired using a good solid grip and your arms at full extension (both techniques combining to manage your firearm's recoil as much as possible), you'd be able to press the trigger as fast as humanly possible, and accurately deliver, well, a lot of rounds in that same three seconds.

So if we agree that the primary purpose of a solid grip is to create and maintain control of the firearm during the firing cycle (thereby allowing the most rapid follow-up shots), then it's going to be important to have as much physical contact between your hands and the firearm as possible, and to do that consistently, as outlined in our step-by-step illustrations. As Pincus explains in his book, *Counter Ambush*, "Consistency is the major factor here. The more consistent your points of contact are with the gun, the more your brain will recognize that you're in the right position to shoot, and the more efficiently you will be at shooting."

SHOOTING STANCE

It's often said that the only "perfect" shooting stance occurs at the range, and that during an actual violent encounter, we'll have to learn to shoot from whatever awkward position we find ourselves in, which might include being seated, rapidly retreating, or lying flat on our back. Because of that, it's best to think of the shooting and "ready" positions discussed in this section as flexible—in other words, while we might prefer using a perfect Isosceles stance at the range, in a real-world situation (or a realistic range exercise or virtual simulation), we might find ourselves in a situation where the only way we can put rounds where we need to, is to use a stance that looks like some strange amalgamation of the Weaver, the Isosceles, and the High Ready position. That's actually okay—if we've trained on the variety of body and arm positions discussed in this section, we can easily transition from one body position to another when the situation calls for it, and still attain a high degree of accuracy, even if we never quite achieve the "perfect" stance.

"READY" POSITIONS

Once the firearm is out of the holster, its appropriate position and orientation are going to depend upon the disposition of the attacker, and the location of loved ones or other friendlies. The two "ready" or "safe" positions shown here and on the opposite page, including the **Low Ready**, and the **High Ready**, are designed for a variety of situations where it is appropriate to have the firearm out of the holster, but where it is *not* yet appropriate to take up a shooting stance, or to reholster. Regardless of the position, the trigger finger should remain *outside* of the trigger guard. From either of these ready positions, we can quickly transition to a shooting stance, or we can reholster if the threat has passed.

Low Ready The low ready position squares the body to the target, with the firearm in a proper grip (and the finger outside the trigger guard) pointed to the ground. This position allows the defender to evaluate the situation while maintaining tight control over his firearm, and allows him to rapidly bring the firearm into action if required.

High Ready The high ready is similar to the low ready, but it draws the firearm into a much tighter retention position against the body. The arms are tightly tucked in against the sides and the muzzle is pointed down. If required, the defender can punch the arms out to full extension, quickly achieving a shooting stance.

Jack Weaver

The Weaver stance was developed by L.A. Deputy Sheriff Jack Weaver, in an effort to win Jeff Cooper's "Leatherslap" competition in Big Bear, California in 1959. At that time, the typical competitive shooter shot from the hip or one-handed from the shoulder, and according to Jack, "What started out as serious business soon produced gales of laughter from the spectators as most of the shooters blazed away..." and "with guns empty and all 12 rounds gone but the 18-inch balloons still standing, they had a problem: load one round and take aim or load six and blaze away again." By the time the 1959 Leatherslap rolled around, Jack had realized that "A pretty quick hit was better than a lightning-fast miss," and decided to bring the pistol up using both hands and use the pistol's sights, rather than just shooting from the hip. Jeff Cooper commented, "Jack walloped us all, decisively. He was very quick and he did not miss." Jack died in April of 2009. One of our most prized possessions is an autographed poster of Jack, showing him at the now famous Leatherslap competition.

WEAVER STANCE

The Weaver stance, named after the late Jack Weaver and taught for nearly four decades at police academies across the world, takes up a "bladed" body position, with the strong side foot placed to the rear and the body bladed at approximately 45 degrees. The theory behind the Weaver stance was that the isometric pressure between the two arms helps to manage recoil, and it places the firearm in a position that allows the shooter to easily focus on the front sight. The problem is, a decade of dash cam videos has proven that regardless of how often police officers had trained on the Weaver, the body's and the mind's natural reaction to face the attacker head on with the arms at full extension took over during actual critical incidents. That evidence was enough to cause most police academies (and most civilian schools) to gravitate toward the more natural and neutral Isosceles stance.

While the Weaver stance looks pretty cool, a decade of dash cam videos has proven that during dynamic critical incidents, we'll be more likely to take up a stance that matches the body's and mind's natural reaction to face the attacker head on, with the arms at full extension.

What's Arc of Movement?

Watch any movie where a laser sight is being used and the red dot doesn't waver a millimeter once it's on target. If you're the Terminator it might work that way, but in real life it doesn't. The body's natural movement, including heartbeat and breathing, and the effects of adrenaline on your muscles, will limit your ability to hold your firearm perfectly on target and a small amount of waver is expected. That's actually okay—at close distances (15 feet or less) a small amount of waver still allows accurate point shooting. In the calculated groupings on the opposite page, we're showing an arc of movement of three degrees, which equates to your muzzle wavering by an inch and a half in any direction, which is exactly the size of a silver dollar. Double the waver and you'll double the margin of error.

person's margin of error with point shooting will deviate by only a few degrees from his or her natural point of aim, allowing for tight shot groups at 10 to 15 feet, and even tighter groups at closer distances. Finally, think

about point shooting in the same way you "shoot" a squirt gun—you don't use the squirt gun's sights and yet, more often than not, you can hit your "target" center of mass.

Whether we're pointing a finger, pointing a dart gun, or pointing a firearm, the human body is *designed* to point. With the arm, hand and finger at full extension, the body has a natural, straight line from the shoulder to the fingertip, and we're born with the ability to point that straight line with a high degree of accuracy. When pointing a firearm, we should train to elevate the firearm up into our line of sight (regardless of our method of target alignment), which allows even more accurate pointing than if the firearm is below our line of sight. When point shooting, the firearm's sights will be out of focus, but should be visible on our target's center of mass. Transitioning between point shooting and sighted fire (when our brain allows us) is then a matter of changing our focus from the target to the front sight.

FLASH SIGHT PICTURE

When the situation we find ourselves in pushes the requirements away from speed and toward accuracy, it will be necessary to use our firearm's sights to achieve a more precise shot. To do that, three indexes must be aligned—the front sight, the rear sight, and the target. But as as mentioned, the automated responses experienced during a violent attack may literally force our eyes to lock on the attacker, making it difficult (or impossible) to focus on the front sight. However, if we've trained ourselves to elevate the firearm up into our line-of-sight, it may be possible to at least gain what's referred to as a "flash sight picture." Put simply, a flash sight picture occurs when the shooter is able to get a rapid "overlay" of the sights on the target, without focusing on the front sight, and without taking the time to gain perfect sight alignment. A flash sight picture will have the target in perfect focus, with the front sight and rear sight both

Flash Sight Picture

A "flash sight picture" occurs when the shooter is able to get a rapid "overlay" of the sights on the target, without focusing on the front sight, and without taking the time to gain perfect sight alignment. The shooter looks for a "flash" of the sights on the target, to verify proper alignment, rather than using the sights to gain proper alignment.

visible (but out of focus) on the target. Said another way, the shooter looks for a "flash" of the sights on the target to *verify* proper alignment, rather than using the sights to *attain* proper alignment. As mentioned earlier, it's important to look at the *exact spot* where you want the round to impact. Then, when the firearm is elevated into your line of sight, a "flash sight picture" occurs (the front and rear sights overlay the spot that you want to shoot) and the trigger is pressed.

SIGHTED FIRE

The most precise shot will require that you switch your focus from the target (where the brain and eyes will want to focus), to the front sight. This is the best method to ensure proper sight alignment. When focused on the front sight, it will be in complete focus, the rear sight will be semi-blurred, and the target will be the blurriest thing in your sight picture. When targets are up close (10—15 feet), misaligned sights

Sighted Fire: Front Sight Focus
When the requirements for precision require that you must use sighted fire, it's important to focus on the front sight rather than the target for the most precise shot. The front sight will be in complete focus, the rear sight will be semi-blurred, and the target will be the blurriest thing in your sight picture.

are more forgiving, but as your target pushes out beyond point shooting distances, even an error of 1/16 of an inch will translate to more than 12-inches of error at 50 feet. Double the error in sight alignment (or double the distance), and you'll double the error on target. What's the best way to ensure perfect sight alignment? See the previous page.

Sighted Fire: Sight Alignment
Equal amounts of spacing should be visible on the left and right of the front sight.

Sights must be in a perfect horizontal line.

At 10–15 feet, these misaligned sights can still mean a hit, but an alignment error as small as 1/16 of an inch will translate to more than 12-inches of error at 50 feet.

TRIGGER CONTROL

When learning any new skill, the mind can typically focus on a single task at a time (it's the old "patting the head while rubbing the stomach" problem). That means that a new shooter, who is focusing on trigger press, might find it difficult to maintain target alignment, and vice-versa. To solve that problem, new shooters should begin with what's known as a "surprise break" when learning proper trigger control. The theory behind the "surprise break" method is that it forces the mind to choose which of the two actions we'll focus on, by choosing to maintain target alignment, rather than focusing on the exact moment that the hammer/striker will fall (think of it as focusing on patting the head, rather than rubbing the stomach). When starting out, we recommend that you begin with the "surprise break" exercise described below, before progressing to the "compressed break" exercise, which will slowly begin to pick up the speed of the trigger press, while maintaining perfect target alignment.

Surprise Break

Gently apply pressure until all of the slack (what's called "take-up") is taken out of the trigger. Counting up to five, continue to apply smooth pressure until the hammer/striker falls (it doesn't matter if the hammer/striker falls at one, at five, or anywhere in between). One-hundred percent of your focus should be on maintaining target alignment, and not on when the hammer/striker falls.

Compressed Break

Gently apply pressure until all of the slack is taken out of the trigger. Counting "one-one-thousand,"

continue to apply smooth pressure until the hammer/striker falls. As with the surprise break, one-hundred percent of your focus should be on maintaining target alignment, and not on when the hammer/striker falls. Continue practicing this drill until the compressed break is reduced below one-half, then one-quarter of a second.

The trigger finger should fall naturally on the trigger, with the trigger centered between the finger tip and first knuckle, or nestled within the crease of the first knuckle (which is called the distal joint). If the finger doesn't fall naturally in this range, the grips are too big or too small.

Finger Tip

Finger Pad

Distal Joint (also called the "Power Crease")

Wherever the trigger is placed, the finger must be pressed STRAIGHT to the rear so that the muzzle alignment is not disturbed.

THE "RUBBER BAND EXERCISE"

The "Rubber Band Exercise" is a simple drill to demonstrate and practice a smooth trigger press from start to finish. Since a rubber band offers smooth resistance with no increase or decrease in resistance, it affords a simple method to practice your trigger press over and over again, while concentrating on a smooth trigger finger movement. For a range exercise to test out how smooth your trigger press actually is, check out the "Ten-to-the-One" drill in Chapter Seven.

◀ The setup for the "Rubber Band Exercise" is simple—it's the same setup you'd use when shooting a rubber band across the room. In this case however, you'll simply flex your trigger finger from a starting point of 90-degrees, and end with it at approximately 60-degrees. Concentrating on a smooth, even "trigger press," will build those neural pathways, and will translate to the range.

TRIGGER RESET

As important as it is to build "muscle memory" for a smooth trigger press that doesn't disrupt target alignment, it's equally important to understand how far forward your trigger must travel before the trigger is reset, and to build that reset point into your neural pathways. The reset point is easily identifiable by a tactile and audible "click" as the trigger is traveling forward. At that reset point, the trigger can once again be pressed to fire the gun. You'll find dramatic differences in how far forward the trigger must travel before it's reset when comparing different types of firearm actions, so you'll need to learn the reset point for each firearm you own. The illustrations to the right provide an example of a Glock, including the trigger position when fully at rest, at the break point (when the gun fires), and at the reset point.

At Rest
The trigger is fully forward.

Break Point
The point at which the striker is released, and the gun fires.

Reset Point
The trigger resets at this point, and can be pressed again, without letting the trigger travel all the way forward to the rest position.

EQUAL·JUST

THE LEGAL USE OF FORCE

» Reviewing the Legal Definitions of
Reasonable Force and Deadly Force

» Understanding the Use of Force Continuum

» A Detailed Walkthrough of the Four Pillars
for Justifying the Use of Deadly Force

» How Defense in the Home Differs
from Outside the Home

» Defending Property

Every state in the U.S. has definitions, statutes, and case law defining when civilians may legally use force (up to and including deadly force) to protect themselves, their families, and their homes. Although statutes and case law vary from state to state, most laws are based at least in part on the "reasonable person" test discussed in Chapter One. That means that whenever any level of force has been used, the prosecutor may second guess your decision, using 12 jurors to decide whether or not they believed your actions were reasonable under the circumstances. We'll start this chapter by looking at our "Use of Force Continuum," which provides examples of escalating levels of force that might be used when defending ourselves from a violent attack. As you'll see on the continuum, each progressive level of force will be viewed with a higher level of scrutiny. Depending upon the circumstances, a jury might decide that it would have been reasonable for you to point your firearm at an attacker, but it was unreasonable to shoot and kill him. When deadly force has been used, in addition to the "reasonableness" test, the courts will ask the jury to ensure that you've met other requirements which we'll also discuss in this chapter.

In addition to discussing your right to use force outside of your home, we'll also discuss your right to use force (up to and including deadly force) when defending your home. This aspect of the law is getting a fresh look in many states. To date, 26 states have passed what are generally referred to as enhanced "Castle Doctrine" laws, which in part, remove the obligation to retreat or escape when you're in a place where you have a right to be; and, they make the legal presumption that someone who has entered your home or occupied vehicle by stealth or force is there to do you harm, allowing you to use deadly force to stop that individual. Since not all states have passed strengthened Castle Doctrine laws, we've included the "obligation to retreat" in our topic on a use of force outside the home.

>> The four deadly force rules must be in place during every single moment when you attempt to use deadly force. As scary and as threatening as this individual looks, count on the prosecutor to second guess your decision whenever deadly force is used.

» Pulling into your apartment complex, you notice a neighbor standing on his third floor balcony.

» You exit your vehicle and head toward the front door of your first floor apartment.

» Leaning over his balcony, your neighbor (who has threatened you in the past) pulls a knife from his waistband and shouts, "You're a dead man!"

» Fearing death or great bodily harm, you shoot your neighbor.

While you could claim that you feared death or great bodily harm, you'd fail on the "immediate" portion of this rule. Since your neighbor was on the third floor and you were on the first, the threat most likely would not be perceived as "immediate" by the prosecutor.

1 REASONABLY IN IMMEDIATE FEAR OF DEATH OR GREAT/GRAVE BODILY HARM FOR YOURSELF OR ANOTHER PERSON

What it Usually Means:

» You must pass the reasonable person test. The prosecutor must agree that a "reasonable person" would have also felt that he or she would have been in immediate fear of death or great/grave bodily harm in the same situation.

» This rule applies whether protecting yourself or another person.

» The threat must be immediate. The attacker must have the *immediate means* and opportunity to carry out his threat. A verbal threat to injure or kill you is not enough.

» Great or grave bodily harm is a legal measurement that implies injuries so great that death is likely or possible, or that you'll be disfigured or crippled permanently or for a significant period of time.

» The condition of the victim matters. For example, in most cases, if a smaller man is punching a larger man in the chest, it would not be considered great/grave bodily harm. However, if the larger man had a pacemaker, the criteria might be met, even though the attacker had no knowledge of the condition.

What it Usually Doesn't Mean:

» It is not necessary that the attacker(s) have a weapon. Depending on the relative number, size and/or strength of the attacker(s) and the victim (what would be called a "disparity of force") the measurement of great/grave bodily harm might be met even though the attacker is unarmed.

» Distance is not critical. If you cannot retreat, you are not required to wait until an attacker is close enough to injure or kill you before you are authorized to use deadly force. Remember the "Tueller Drill" (and remind your lawyer about it).

2 MUST BE AN INNOCENT PARTY

What it Usually Means:
» In a deadly force situation, you must be the innocent party—you *cannot* be seen as the aggressor. That is, you must not be the person who started or escalated the conflict.

» Shoving someone at a bar obviously violates this rule, but how about flipping someone off on the freeway? If the situation escalates, don't be so sure what the prosecutor will think.

» The prosecutor will not only analyze the timeline of the incident itself, he'll also want to go back in time before the incident occurred to understand whether or not you knew the attacker, whether there was bad blood between you, and if there are any witnesses or evidence (prior arrests, etc.) to suggest that you're not as innocent as you claim to be.

What it Usually Doesn't Mean:
» It doesn't mean that you are barred from everyday disagreements, but it does mean that if you see the situation escalating, you must disengage, allowing the situation to de-escalate.

» You are not barred from coming to the defense of another person, but unless you can clearly identify who is the attacker and who is the innocent victim, a prudent course of action would be to call 911 and be a good witness. Don't assume that the guy who has the upper hand in the fight is the bad guy.

» After entering a bar, another individual steps on your toe.

» You mutter "asshole" under your breath.

> You failed the "innocent party" rule.

» The individual bumps into your shoulder, knocking you back.

» You shove the individual to the floor.

> You failed the "innocent party" rule again.

» The individual jumps up from the floor and charges you with a knife.

> At this point, you are in immediate risk of death or great bodily harm, but since you've broken rule #2, you should expect to be charged with a crime.

» You shoot the individual charging you with the knife.

SCENARIO #3

» You leave a busy city street and turn down an alley to take a shortcut to your car.

» An individual approximately half your size steps from behind a dumpster and pulls his shirt aside, while reaching for a semi-automatic tucked into his waistband.

» You shout, "don't hurt me!" and draw your firearm from the holster. You leave your pepper spray in your pocket.

» The individual draws his firearm from his waistband, and elevates it in an effort to shoot you.

» You fire two rounds at him and one strikes him in the shoulder. He immediately drop his firearm and it slides under the dumpster.

» Bleeding, the individual stumbles toward you.

» The individual refuses your further commands to stay back, and he steps into what you consider to be your "danger zone" so you shoot him again.

Your first mistake. While you haven't broken one of the rules yet, you've put yourself in a risky situation that could have been avoided if you'd stayed with the crowds.

At this point, you would probably get most prosecutors to agree that you had no alternative other than to immediately resort to deadly force, and that you would not have been expected to try your pepper spray first.

However, at this point, the individual no longer had control of his firearm (and was injured) and your pepper spray would most likely have sufficed to have stopped the continued threat. In addition, a prosecutor might argue that you've also broken rules #1 and #4 as well.

3 NO LESSER FORCE IS SUFFICIENT OR AVAILABLE TO STOP THE THREAT

What it Usually Means:
» If you can stop a threat with something less than deadly force, you are required to. For example, if a reasonable person would have expected that you could have stopped an attack with your hands (or the pepper spray that you chose to carry) the prosecutor may not agree that deadly force was authorized.

» You are required to stop using deadly force as soon as the threat of death or great/grave bodily harm has ended. If three bullets stop an attack, the fourth bullet could be considered a crime.

» Relative size and strength of the attacker(s) and/or victim matter. For example, a large man being attacked by an unarmed, much smaller woman, may have lesser-force alternatives rather than resorting to deadly force. In the reverse scenario, the disparity of force may mean that the smaller woman might have no alternative other than immediately resorting to deadly force.

What it Usually Doesn't Mean:
» You are not required to try other methods before using deadly force, you are simply expected to consider alternatives, and to only use deadly force when no other option is sufficient or available.

MUST HAVE NO REASONABLE MEANS OF RETREAT OR ESCAPE

What it Usually Means:

» Many states' laws require that if you can do so safely, you are expected to seek escape from a potential attack (if an avenue of escape is available and practical), before standing your ground and defending yourself with deadly force.

» Reasons for an inability to retreat or escape can include: The attacker has physical control over you, and you are simply unable to escape; the attacker is already too close, and you have no ability to outrun them; the attacker has a firearm, and it would be impossible to try to "outrun the bullet;" or you are in a location which offers no ability to escape, such as a room where the attacker is blocking the exit.

» The obligation to retreat never ends. For example, if you are able to wound an attacker such that it opens up an opportunity to escape safely, you must retreat at that point.

What it Usually Doesn't Mean:

» The "escape" rule doesn't mean that you cannot have been traveling in a forward direction at any point during the timeline (for example, it doesn't bar you from moving toward a person whom you believe has committed, or is about to commit a crime, although it's good *practical* advice to avoid that type of situation), it simply means that at the moment a threat materializes, if you still have an ability to escape the situation, you *should* escape.

» You are not expected to retreat from a bad situation to a worse one. For example, if your only means of retreat is across a busy road, you are not expected to put yourself in greater danger by retreating.

» You are not expected to retreat and leave behind a companion in the dangerous situation. That is, if you can outrun the attacker, you are not expected to do so if it means leaving a companion behind.

SCENARIO #4

» On your way home from work, a dog runs in front of your car on the freeway. You slam on your brakes and are rear ended.

» Your car is fine, so you continue on until you can pull onto the shoulder, but the other car is out of commission, and pulls over several hundred feet behind you.

» The other individual jumps out of his car with a machete, and charges your vehicle, screaming that he's going to kill you.

» You exit your vehicle, and take up a position behind your driver's door. You shout commands continuously for the 40 seconds it takes the other individual to reach you.

» You shoot the individual as he gets within 20 feet of you.

At this point, you are in immediate risk of death or great bodily harm, but you had plenty of time to drive off (remember that your car was fine in this scenario), leaving the deranged individual behind.

HOW WILL THE PROSECUTOR EVALUATE YOUR CASE?

As discussed in Chapter One, when deciding whether or not to file charges against an individual claiming self–defense, the prosecutor is going to care about more than just who was shot and who did the shooting. As outlined in our scenarios, the prosecutor will analyze each time slice of the incident in an attempt to understand exactly what occurred, including whether or not you started the ball rolling or kept it rolling. The prosecutor might also back up to the hours, days, and even years before the incident, in an attempt to understand the entire story. The prosecutor will want to know:

» Does the timeline include anything that shows you as the aggressor (even if it happened after an initial move by the other individual)? In other words, did you start the ball rolling, or give it a good kick to keep it rolling?

» Did you know the other individual, and was there any history of bad blood? How far back does the timeline extend?

» What kind of individual are you? What do your friends, ex-friends, neighbors, and co-workers say about you?

» What's on your Facebook page, including pictures, philosophy, and behavior? Is there any indication of aggressiveness, a belief in vigilantism, or gang activity?

» Are you considered a bully or aggressive? Are there any witnesses, prior arrests, or documentation (including anything you've ever written, posted, emailed, blogged, texted, or tweeted) that would substantiate that categorization?

» Did you pass or fail the "reasonable person" test, including whether or not you used a reasonable level of force based upon the circumstances?

» Do they believe that you met all four deadly force criteria during *every single moment* of the timeline where you threatened deadly force?

» Was any alcohol in your blood, and if so, does that affect your "reasonable person" argument?

» What statements did you make to the police immediately after the incident? (The answer to this question better be nothing.)

» What did the police uncover during a search of your car or home? (Any search better have been conducted with a warrant, rather than your passive agreement.)

Based upon the answers to those questions, you may not be viewed as the innocent victim. You might be viewed as a hot-headed bully that got the ball rolling, even if the "ball" got rolling months in advance. Here's the reality—in the end, it truly doesn't matter what *really* happened. What matters is what the prosecutor can get 12 people to believe. If your past behavior leads the jury to agree with the prosecutor's version of events, even an incident where you did

» If the prosecutor isn't buying your story, he's going to give you a chance
to sell it to 12 jurors, who most decidedly will not be your peers. Don't
count on any permit holders or lifetime NRA members to sit on your jury.

» If this burglar hasn't yet entered the home, do the deadly force rules outside the home, or inside the home apply? Don't be so sure what the prosecutor will think.

everything right might result in your conviction, since your attacker will have his own version of events which might include, "This crazy dude pulled a gun on me, so I had to pull my knife to defend myself!" Who will the prosecutor and/or jury believe?

Our best advice? Be nice to everyone; be smart about alcohol use; and don't ever say, email, text, or post anything that could help a prosecutor's case. To quote Mother Teresa, "Treat people with more kindness than is required." While you can't get Mother Teresa to testify on your behalf, her philosophy might help you in the end.

Using Deadly Force to Defend Your Home

State laws governing the use of deadly force in defense of our homes (or defense of ourselves or our families while in our homes) generally provide a lower threshold when compared to the lawful use of deadly force outside the home. That difference is derived from the belief that "our home is our castle," and laws making that distinction are often referred to as Castle Doctrine laws (which as mentioned in the chapter introduction, are being strengthened in a number of states). While the generally accepted rule for the use of deadly force outside the home is to prevent "death or great/grave bodily harm," most state laws authorize a use of force deadly inside the home when the occupant is attempting to end or prevent a felony in the home. What exactly a "felony" is will vary from state to state, and of course, the prosecutor gets to apply his or her interpretation after the fact. Most states also make a distinction between inside and outside the home when it comes to the requirement to retreat. Outside the home, many states still require the potential victim to retreat if retreat is safe and practical; inside the home, that is generally not a requirement.

When it comes to the applicability of "defense of home" laws versus the general use of force laws, state laws also vary when it comes to defining exactly what the "home" is. Some states will only include the physical structure of your home or apartment, while other states may include detached buildings (such as garages or storage sheds) and others will include any location where you spend the night, such as a hotel, motel, tent, camper, etc. Because of the variety of state laws, and the fact that the "reasonable person" test will usually apply in any defense of home claim, we recommend that you do the following when defending your home:

» If an intruder is in the home, do *not* attempt to locate him by "clearing rooms." Instead, barricade yourself and your family in a safe location, call 911, and defend that safe location. There is one time and one time *only* that you should even consider advancing through your home to clear a room or rooms, and that's when the bad guy is between you and a loved one. Otherwise you should concentrate your energy on defending your safe zone until the police arrive.

» If an intruder is outside of your home, in your garage, in your storage shed, or attempting to steal your car, do *not* leave your home in an attempt to stop him. Call 911 and only use force to defend your life or the lives of your family.

WHAT ABOUT USING FORCE TO DEFEND PROPERTY?

While most states' laws allow a use of force to protect property (or to keep it from being stolen) they typically do not allow a use of deadly force. The problem is, if you voluntarily step into a situation with the intent to use force to protect property, and the situation escalates to the point where you are forced to use deadly force to protect yourself, the prosecutor could argue that you violated the "innocent party" rule, or, they could argue that you used deadly force to protect the property (which is *not* okay) rather than your life (which *is* okay). Because of that, our recommendation is that you not use force to protect property, instead, we recommend that you get to a safe location or *stay* in a safe location, and dial 911.

To illustrate the differences between a "defense of property" and a "defense of person," many instructors use the "shark tank" analogy. The analogy asks us, "What would it take for me to jump into a shark tank? How about if my child fell in?" For most parents, it wouldn't even be a question—they'd jump into the tank in an attempt to rescue their child, even if they knew it could mean their death. The analogy goes on to ask, "Would I jump in to save an expensive watch?" You get the difference? If it isn't worth dying over, then it isn't worth killing over. Dial 911, and stay safe.

» Although most states' laws allow a use of force to stop property crimes, they typically do not allow deadly force. If it isn't worth dying over, and if it isn't worth going to jail over, then it isn't worth using (or threatening) deadly force. Call 911 and be a good witness instead.

CHAPTER 5

VIOLENT ENCOUNTERS AND THEIR AFTERMATH

In Chapter Three, we briefly mentioned a number of "automated responses" that typically accompany what is generally referred to as a "critical incident," which is an antiseptic way of referring to a violent attack. We explained that those automated responses would most likely include the motor cortex locking your head and eyes onto the knife or gun in the hands of the attacker; and the automated response of dropping into a crouch, and orienting to face the attacker. In this chapter, we'll not only explain more details around those *physical* responses, we'll also explain a number of *physiological* responses that will most likely occur as well, including tunnel vision, auditory exclusion, and even memory loss or false memories. To do that, we're going to take you on a guided tour of the brain and nervous system, where we'll explain not only *what* responses you'll most likely experience, but we'll explain *why*

they happen as well. As you read that section, pay particularly close attention to the "Training Tips" that we've outlined for each topic. These tips are designed to help you embrace each of the physical and physiological responses into your training plan in order to "train the way you'll fight."

Also in this chapter, we'll review what you should do in the opening stages of an attack, including reviewing what your options might be, and the type of language and commands to use (and not to use). We'll also address the very difficult topic of exactly what you'll need to know if you have no other choice but to use deadly force to stop an attack.

We'll also explain what you should do in the immediate aftermath of an attack, including what phone calls you should make, how to deal with the police when they arrive at the scene, and what you should and shouldn't say to the police. It's unfortunate, but the reality is that if you've used your firearm in any capacity, however justified you believed it to be, the police are no longer there to serve and protect you. They are there to serve the prosecuting attorney and protect his or her case. For that reason, you'll need to prepare for how to interact with the police after such an incident, including preparing for your arrest. We'll help by explaining exactly what might happen after your arrest, including an explanation of when the police are required to read the famous (or infamous) Miranda warning, reminding you of your right to remain silent. We'll explain what that warning really means, and we'll also explain what you'll need to do to actually invoke that right (believe it or not, you can't invoke the right to remain silent by simply being silent). It's an unfortunate reality, but once a "critical incident" has ended, the real trouble is just getting started.

THE BRAIN AND CENTRAL NERVOUS SYSTEM

The brain is made up of a variety of interconnected structures, but the ones we'll concentrate on are those involved in sensory input and sensory processing, reasoning and planning, movement, and the brain's "alarm circuits." We'll also take a look at a key component of the nervous system called the sympathetic nervous system. To make it a bit easier to understand, we're going to use everyday descriptive terms (such as "the Switchboard") in addition to using the technical term (such as "the thalamus").

The "Switchboard"

Our senses (things like sight, sound, and touch) provide sensory and emotional input to our brains, which is routed through a structure called the **thalamus**. The thalamus used to be thought of as nothing more than a relay station, simply passing signals from the senses to the sensory cortex. Now, scientists think of the thalamus as more of a "switchboard" within the brain, making determinations about where input is routed, and which information is filtered or blocked. As it receives sensory input, the thalamus routes that input to the cortex (the long route) and the amygdala (the short route). Under periods of extreme stress, scientists believe that the thalamus can block any sensory input that it doesn't consider necessary to the situation.

The "Thinker"

The cortex not only allows us to plan and reason, it also contains sub-structures to interpret sensory input that has been routed from the thalamus. Like the thalamus (the "Switchboard"), the **sensory cortex** will selectively process or ignore input based upon the task at hand. For example, when we're focused on a TV program (visual input) we don't always hear our spouse's request to take out the garbage; or, when we're focused on a radio program in the car (audio input), we might ignore the visual input of a stop sign and blow right by it. When we're under extreme stress, this selective processing and prioritization becomes pronounced.

The "Engineer"

The **motor cortex** receives most of its instructions from the thinking and planning part of our brain, but the amygdala also has a direct connection to the motor cortex for those times when it's necessary for us to do something *right now*, such as freezing, ducking, raising our hands, or crouching.

The "Fire Alarm"

Sitting next to the thalamus is a tiny, almond-shaped structure called the **amygdala**. The amygdala contains most of the brain's alarm circuits designed to react to any imminent threat passed on by the thalamus. When its alarm circuits are tripped, the amygdala has a direct connection to the motor cortex (that is, it skips the reasoning and planning part of the brain) in order to take *immediate* action (such as making us duck if something is thrown at our heads), and to the hypothalamus, to kick our endocrine system into gear. "Evolved" alarms are contained within the amygdala, such as a fear of large, roaring carnivores, while "learned" alarms are accessed by the hippocampus (the "Scrapbook") such as a fear of snakes with rattles.

The "Scrapbook"

The **hippocampus** provides access to our memories and personal experiences, including any "learned" threats. That recall will include more than just a visual snapshot of the learned threat, it will also recall information about the context and situation surrounding the object. For example, if an individual had been attacked by a thug wielding a baseball bat, the sight of another individual carrying a baseball bat might fire the alarm circuits if the rest of the context met other stored criteria, such as an aggressive facial expression on the part of the person with the bat. On the other hand, a baseball bat in the hands of a smiling little leaguer most likely would not fire those circuits.

The "Pharmacy"

The sympathetic nervous system involves two additional structures in the brain, namely the **hypothalamus** and the **pituitary gland**, as well as the **adrenal glands**, situated on top of the kidneys. Upon hearing the alarm bells fired by the amygdala, the hypothalamus signals the pituitary gland to release ACTH and endorphins. ACTH alerts the adrenal glands to release adrenaline (also known as epinephrine) into the bloodstream, and endorphins act as a natural pain killer by blocking the body's pain receptors.

UNDERSTANDING FIGHT OR FLIGHT

It's been long known that when under extreme stress (including when under attack) the human body will undergo a series of involuntary changes as part of the "fight or flight" mechanisms built into our systems. Anecdotal evidence from the last five wars plus a number of law enforcement studies, have all confirmed that these effects happen, yet very few delve into *why* they happen or *how often* they happen. Three of the leading researchers in this field, including Dr. Alexis Artwohl, Dr. Bill Lewinski, and Bruce Siddle, have finally begun to answer the "why" and the "how often" side of this question, and the answers are truly astounding.

In her book "Deadly Force Encounters" (written with co-author Loren Christensen) and subsequent research papers, Dr. Alexis Artwohl provides incredible insight through in-depth interviews with 157 police officers involved in deadly force shootings. The many quotations you'll see in this section are from Dr. Artwohl's interviews, and a summary of her findings are shown in the chart to the right, which shows that approximately 80% of the officers interviewed experienced the most well-known physiological effects, including tunnel vision and diminished sounds, and that more than 50% experienced time distortions or memory loss. Most surprising, more than one in five experienced false memories; that is, they remembered something that *never actually happened*. These and other physical and physiological effects have long been attributed to adrenaline or other natural chemicals that flood our bodies during extreme stress, but the "fight or flight" mechanisms that are part of our systems go well beyond a simple chemical dump by our adrenal glands. They exist as a true survival mechanism that is hardwired into our brains, as surely as an electronic fuse will trip when a short occurs. Like any electrical system, the brain is composed of an incredibly complex set of relays, switches, and multiple paths that signals can travel down. As explained on the opposite page and as shown on the brain schematic on the following pages, "fight or flight" (and everything that cascades from it), all starts with a tiny, almond shaped structure in the brain called the amygdala.

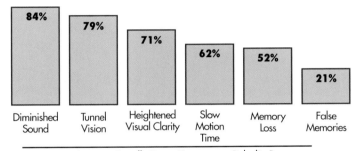

Source: Deadly Force Encounters, Paladin Press
Based on Surveys from 157 Police Officers involved in Deadly Encounters

PHYSIOLOGICAL EFFECTS OF EXTREME STRESS

Effects of the Brain's "Alarm Circuits"
>> Reflexive Crouch.
>> Hands Elevated to Protect the Face.
>> Head Turned and Eyes Locked on Threat.

Effects of Brain's Signals Being Prioritized or Filtered
>> Tunnel Vision.
>> Heightened Visual Clarity.
>> Diminished Sounds.
>> Slow Motion Time.
>> Memory Loss.
>> Memory Distortion or False Memories.
>> Inability to Count.

Effects of Adrenaline and Endorphins
>> Increase in Strength.
>> Heightened Pain Threshold.
>> Decrease in Fine Motor Skills.

THE BRAIN'S LONG ROUTE AND SHORT ROUTE

The body's "fight or flight" defenses are coordinated by a variety of interconnected structures in our brain and sympathetic nervous system, including the structures shown below. The amygdala (the "Fire Alarm") is responsible for initiating the body's "fight or flight" defenses whenever it receives sensory input that matches predefined alarm circuits. Sensory input reaches the amygdala from the thalamus (the "Switchboard") along two paths. One path is a direct connection, while the second path is first routed through the sensory cortex (the "Thinker"). The route through the cortex is known as the long route or the higher brain, while the direct connection is known as the short route or the reptilian brain. Although input is passed from the thalamus along both paths, in most cases, the lower brain remains passive, and our

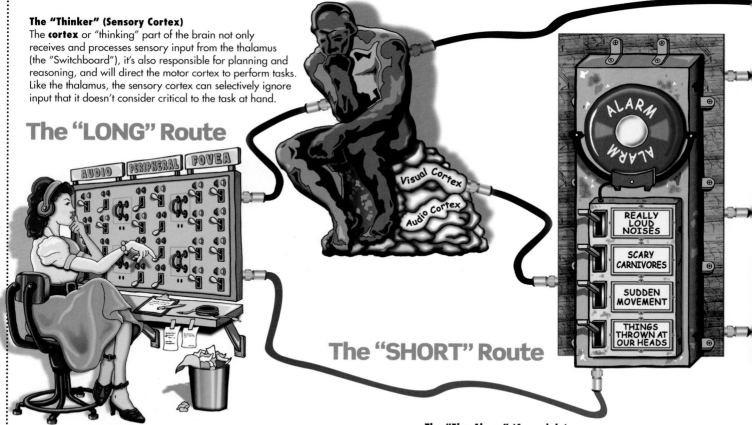

The "Thinker" (Sensory Cortex)
The **cortex** or "thinking" part of the brain not only receives and processes sensory input from the thalamus (the "Switchboard"), it's also responsible for planning and reasoning, and will direct the motor cortex to perform tasks. Like the thalamus, the sensory cortex can selectively ignore input that it doesn't consider critical to the task at hand.

The "LONG" Route

The "SHORT" Route

The "Switchboard" (Thalamus)
The **thalamus** can be thought of as the switchboard of the brain, responsible for routing, blocking, or filtering sensory input. In the illustration above, the thalamus has blocked nearly all audio and visual input other than the high resolution fovea at the center of the retina.

The "Fire Alarm" (Amygdala)
The **amygdala** contains the brain's hardwired alarm circuits which will fi[...] if matching input is received from the thalamus, such as a really loud noi[...] (watch any video of soldiers ducking when a mortar shell goes off, and y[...] just saw the amygdala in action) or when something is thrown at our hea[...]

movement and other activity is driven by our higher brain as it processes and "thinks about" the input that it's receiving. In cases where the information flowing along the paths matches a predefined alarm circuit, the amygdala effectively throws a switch, and within microseconds, it executes a series of tasks that may include signaling the motor cortex (the "Engineer") to duck into a crouch, rotate toward the perceived threat and lock our eyes on that threat; and it might send a message to the hypothalamus (the "Pharmacy") to get adrenaline moving into the system. Much faster than it would take to think through the situation, the short path through our brain has already prepared us for fight or flight, and it might have already saved us from serious injury or death if it froze our motor cortex before we stepped in front of a speeding bus, or ducked our head to protect us from a flying rock.

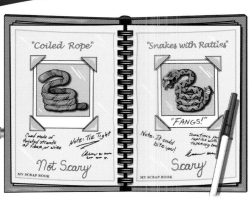

The "Scrapbook" (Hippocampus)

The **hippocampus** provides access to our memories and experiences, including any "learned" threats and the context surrounding those threats. For example, the hippocampus could access the fact that coiled objects are threats if they're alive and have rattles, but that coiled objects that look like rope are not threats. When matching threat information is identified by the hippocampus, the amygdala will fire its alarm bells.

The "Engineer" (Motor Cortex)

The amygdala has a direct connection to the **motor cortex** for those moments when we need to do something immediately, such as: freezing; raising our hands to protect our head from a flying rock; or ducking into a crouch, orienting toward a threat, and locking our eyes onto that threat.

The "Pharmacy" (Hypothalamus, Pituitary Gland & Adrenal Gland)

Upon hearing the alarm bells fired by the amygdala, the **hypothalamus** signals the **pituitary gland** to release ACTH and endorphins. ACTH alerts the **adrenal glands** to release adrenaline (also known as epinephrine) into the bloodstream, and endorphins act as a natural pain killer by blocking the body's pain receptors.

TRAINING TIP

>> Since the amygdala's direct connection to the motor cortex will force you into a crouch and will orient your body to face the threat head on, then that's the "stance" you should train with. The Isosceles is a natural and neutral stance, matching the body's and mind's

ADRENALINE & ENDORPHINS

As discussed, the amygdala is responsible for *initiating* the body's "fight or flight" defenses, while the sympathetic nervous system is responsible for *sustaining* it through a release of adrenaline. Adrenaline sustains the body's "fight or flight" defenses by increasing blood, oxygen, and glucose to the major muscles including the heart; it increases heart rate and oxygen consumption by the lungs, and it dilates the pupils. Side effects will include a loss of manual dexterity in our extremities (most importantly, our hands) and our hands may shake from the loss of blood and the influx of adrenaline. In addition, the lack of blood on the surface of our skin and the effect of endorphins released by the pituitary gland will provide us with an elevated pain threshold.

This can allow us to fight long after we might have given up from injuries, but it also means that we'll need to immediately check ourselves and loved ones for injuries in the immediate aftermath.

Under Stress
Adrenaline forces a constriction of blood vessels to force blood, oxygen, and glucose to the major muscle groups and away from the skin and extremities to allow us to run faster than we've ever run, or fight harder than we've ever fought.

No Stress
When relaxed, the muscles have an equal distribution of blood, oxygen and glucose. The major muscle groups have normal strength and the minor muscle groups have high dexterity.

The manual dexterity that we'll lose under the effects of adrenaline just happens to be the same dexterity required to manipulate holster retention devices, safeties, and slide releases.

TRAINING TIP

》 Learn to manipulate your firearm's controls as though you were missing your fingertips. That means ignoring your slide release, and racking (or releasing) the slide by grasping it between the palm and four fingers of your support hand. If you want a taste of what your hands might actually feel like under the affects of adrenaline and extreme stress, try this: run through our "Slap, Rack, and Roll Drill" in Chapter Seven, after soaking your hands in a sink full of water and ice cubes for a minute or two. The resulting hand shake and lack of feeling will give you a small taste of the real thing.

THE STRUCTURE OF THE EYE

To understand why visual side effects occur, it's necessary to understand the structure of the eye itself. As shown in the diagram below, the human eye can be thought of as being similar to a digital camera. In a camera, the lens focuses the image onto a CCD chip containing millions of light sensitive cells. In the human eye, the lens focuses the image onto the eye's retina which contains more than 100 million photosensitive cells called rods and cones. Rods and cones convert

the exact center of the retina contains a tiny area called the fovea, composed entirely of the higher resolution cones. Interestingly, the area of the visual cortex that's mapped directly to the fovea is disproportionately large when compared to the area mapped to the remainder of the retina. Said another way, not only does the fovea provide a much higher resolution image when compared to the rest of the eye, but the brain also sets aside a much greater amount of power to process that input. Although the entire retina provides as much as

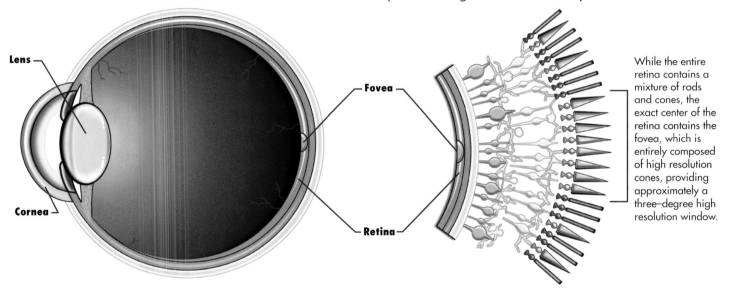

Lens

Cornea

Fovea

Retina

While the entire retina contains a mixture of rods and cones, the exact center of the retina contains the fovea, which is entirely composed of high resolution cones, providing approximately a three–degree high resolution window.

the incoming light into signals which are sent into the visual cortex for processing, via the thalamus (the "Switchboard"). Rods and cones serve different purposes. Rods are designed to operate in low light and they're sensitive to movement, but they see in black and white and are low resolution. Cones provide a much higher resolution image and they see in color, but they are less beneficial in low light. While the majority of the retina has a mixture of rods and cones,

200 degrees of peripheral vision, the higher resolution fovea provides no more than a few degrees of vision. Don't believe it? Try this test—stare at any word on this page and try to identify any other word at least three to four words away. You'll pretty easily see that the word you're focused on looks high resolution, while every other word appears low resolution and is most likely illegible.

TUNNEL VISION AND HEIGHTENED VISUAL CLARITY

So why does tunnel vision and heightened visual clarity occur? As shown in our brain schematic, the thalamus acts as the brain's switchboard, not only deciding *where* to route signals, but also *if* it should route a signal at all. Under extreme stress, the thalamus filters out what it considers to be non-critical sensory input, which may include filtering out visual input other than the information from the eye's high resolution fovea. That means that our visual input might be reduced to no more than a few degrees (which equates to about a 12-inch circle at 20 feet) but the input that is processed, is *extremely* high resolution. That corresponds with reports from survivors of violent attacks who experienced tunnel vision and who often couldn't describe their assailant, but could describe their assailant's weapon in detail, as though they were reviewing a high resolution picture.

DISTANCE DISTORTION

Survivors of critical incidents have also reported distance distortion, either believing that their attacker was much closer or much farther away than he actually was. Tunnel vision can cause us to believe that an attacker was farther away than he actually was, since we're losing most of our stereoscopic vision, which is required for depth perception. The "high resolution effect" or "heightened visual clarity" can lead us to believe the attacker was closer than he actually was, since under normal circumstances, we know the difference between how clear and well-focused a person or object is at different distances. Under the effects of extreme stress, when the brain is limiting the visual input to the high resolution area at the center of the retina, a person who is actually at 20 feet may look like he has the same clarity and detail as a person at, say, 10 feet. Our replay of the incident would incorrectly conclude that the person was closer than he actually was.

> " I told the SWAT team that the suspect was firing at me from down a long dark hallway about 40 feet long. When I went back to the scene the next day, I was shocked to discover that he had actually been only about 5 feet in front of me in an open room. There was no dark hallway. "

Under normal circumstances, the visual cortex is receiving input from the entire retina, which provides up to 200 degrees of vision.

Under extreme stress, the thalamus filters out (or the sensory cortex ignores) visual input from everything but the high resolution fovea, reducing vision to no more than a few degrees, but providing very high resolution images.

TRAINING TIP

>> Take a look through a paper towel tube to get a sense of what the scene will look like with just three degrees of visibility. With that mental picture, train yourself to elevate your firearm up into that three–degree window and physically move your head, rather than just your eyes, when engaging multiple targets. When running drills on the range, practice lowering your firearm to a low ready once the drill is complete, and perform a 360° scan of the area by physically moving your head. In a critical incident, this head movement can reset the filtering that occurs within the thalamus or sensory cortex.

DIMINISHED SOUND (AUDITORY EXCLUSION)

Selective auditory exclusion happens all the time (just try to get the attention of an eight-year-old when he's watching SpongeBob). This is nothing more than the sensory cortex's prioritization of one signal over another, which also explains why we can hold a conversation in a crowded room full of noise. During non-critical moments, we can easily change our sensory focus by listening to a different conversation or temporarily ignoring audio input while we focus on visual input. This is an everyday function of our sensory cortex—it allows us to selectively process sensory input to accomplish the task at hand. However, once the brain's alarm circuits have been fired, the thalamus (the "Switchboard") appears to literally halt the flow of audio signals to the cortex. This corresponds with interviews from the Artwohl research, where police officers who experienced auditory exclusion *knew* their firearms should be going "bang," they were *listening* for their firearms to go "bang," yet all they heard was a "pop" or no sound at all. Interestingly, while the thalamus appears to halt the flow of audio signals along the "long route," it appears as though the signal flow along the "short route" is uninterrupted. In a study conducted by Bruce and Kevin Siddle of PPCT Management Systems in 2004, researchers put 49 police officers in an enclosed trailer, and ran the officers through an intense force-on-force drill, where the officers were fired on from three different "attackers." During the 30 second "attack," the researchers sounded an air horn, which in the enclosed space, should have been deafening. During the debriefing, when the officers were asked if they heard the air horn, fully 97% replied that they *never heard it*. The video tape, however, told a different story—39 percent of the officers who said that they never heard the air horn still reacted to it by flinching, or by briefly orienting toward the sound. That indicates that the thalamus-to-amygdala connection remained in place, which allowed the amygdala to continue its automated processes, even though the "thinking" part of the brain was left out of the loop.

≫ How Does Hearing Protection Compare? Typical ear protection will lower a sound source by approximately 20 to 30 decibels, which means that the "bang" of gunfire might still be as loud as 110 to 120 decibels. Compare that to the reported sound levels from officers in the Artwohl research, where officers reported gunfire sounding like "pops" or no sound at all, and had no recollection of sirens or shouts. That means that the apparent sound reduction was greater than 80 decibels, and as high as 140 decibels.

> *If it hadn't been for the recoil, I wouldn't have known my gun was working. Not only didn't I hear the shots but afterward my ears weren't even ringing.*

Actual Audio Volume

Gunfire
140db

Siren
110db

Shouts
80db

The "Switchboard" (Thalamus)

AUDIO PERIPHERAL FOVEA

» The signals from the thalamus to the sensory cortex can be blocked or filtered by the thalamus; or, they can simply be ignored by the sensory cortex.

Volume Received by Sensory Cortex

Gunfire
0 - 40db

Siren
0db

Shouts
0db

TRAINING TIP

» With a buddy's assistance, try our "Slap, Rack, and Roll Drill" in Chapter Seven, with live stereo ear pieces inserted under your normal hearing protection. Turn up the volume loud enough so that the combination of music and hearing protection drowns out all other sounds. This will teach you to recognize your firearm's proper operation and failures by feel alone. You'll learn to trust that your firearm actually fired even though you didn't hear the "bang," and you'll learn to identify failures through a lack of recoil, rather than a lack of sound.

SLOW MOTION TIME

Processing the input of sensory information requires processing power, no different than a computer requires processing power to run applications. During non-stressful situations, our sensory cortex must balance the processing of a variety of sensory input, including sound, touch, smell, and about 200 degrees of visual input. Under periods of extreme stress when the thalamus has shut down all sensory input except for the high resolution fovea, we'll suddenly have throughput and processing power to spare. So what does that have to do with the "slow motion effect" reported in the Artwohl research? In part, it's due to the fact that most of our perception of time is based upon the sensory input that we receive. Under extreme stress, the unusually high volume of visual information that's passed to and is processed by our cortex can be interpreted by our conscious self as time slowing down, rather than the "processing" or "throughput" speeding up. To use another computer analogy, let's assume that a computer is running ten applications, including a video processing application that

normally processes one gigabyte of video per second. If the other nine applications were suddenly shut down, the computer might suddenly jump to processing 10 gigabytes per second. If the computer's clock was based upon how many gigabytes were processed, it would now record that ten seconds had passed for each real second, which from the computer's perspective, is the most logical conclusion (rather than concluding that its processing power had somehow magically increased). That's an over simplification, but it paints an easy picture to understand.

Five Seconds at Twice the Volume of Visual Input Can be Interpreted by the Mind as Ten Seconds
During periods of extreme stress when the thalamus is blocking virtually all sensory input other than the high resolution fovea, we'll not only have a much wider stream of high resolution visual input, but we'll suddenly have the processing power to handle it. Continuing the analogy to film, it's like jumping from 24 frames per second to 48 frames per second or more. The result can be like something straight out of "The Matrix," such as the amazing quote from the Artwohl research on the opposite page.

> **During a violent shoot-out I looked over, drawn to the sudden mayhem, and was puzzled to see beer cans slowly floating through the air past my face. What was even more puzzling was that they had the word "Federal" printed on the bottom. They turned out to be the shell casings ejected by the officer who was firing next to me.**

Five Seconds of Real Time

Although light enters the eye as a continuous stream and not as individual "frames," the analogy to film helps to explain why slow motion time occurs. During normal, non-stressful situations, the cortex will process a balance of sensory information in order to accomplish the task at hand. Visual processing might be comparable to traditional motion picture film at 24 frames per second. That's enough visual input to walk without tripping over our feet, and to catch a ball without getting hit in the face, yet it's slow enough to cause motion blur. For example, empty shell casings flying by our face will appear as a blur.

TRAINING TIP

» Practice reloads and clearance drills without looking at your firearm. During a critical incident, if your perception is that you're performing these tasks in slow motion, you can rush the task and make mistakes when mistakes can be fatal.

LOSS OF MEMORY

In order to recall a memory, our hippocampus (the "Scrapbook") actually reconstructs it by integrating elements of that memory scattered in various locations of our brain. For example, for us to recall a camping trip from the previous summer, the brain doesn't open a "file" the same way a computer file is opened; instead, the hippocampus reconstructs the memory by recalling separately stored memories connected via pathways of what we did, saw, smelled, tasted, and heard on that trip. Memories are also associative, which means that newer memories are more easily recalled if we can associate them with previously acquired knowledge. For example, if the camping trip reminded us of an earlier trip we'd been on, it would be easier to recall the details of the more recent event. Under extreme stress, we're lacking both of those fundamental "recall" operations. Instead of a variety of elements stored for that memory, we might have only a single element captured (visual) and we most likely have no previous memories to associate it with. In addition, in order to be recalled in the first place, memories must have been transferred to long term memory (also managed by the hippocampus), which required them to be transferred from "sensory memory" (which might last less than a second) to short term or "working" memory (which might last less than a minute), to long term memory. Under extreme stress, the hippocampus may simply discard information that it doesn't consider necessary to survival, never moving the input past sensory or short term memory. The Artwohl research includes multiple incidents where officers blacked out on one or more parts of the incident, including their own actions, such as forgetting phone calls they made, how many rounds they fired, or even whether or not they fired their own gun.

> " When I got home after the shooting, my wife told me that I had called her on my cell phone during the pursuit of the violent suspect just prior to the shooting. I have no memory of making that phone call. "

» If this individual suddenly pulled a knife, what are your options? Do you engage the threat? Take cover? Run in the opposite direction? It's important to remember that in most violent attacks, we have options, but if the option we choose is any level of force, we may need to convince a jury that our decision was reasonable for the circumstances.

ISSUING COMMANDS & EVALUATING OPTIONS

Issuing commands during a violent encounter does two things. Most importantly, it immediately identifies us as someone who will not be an easy victim, which may cause the attacker to break off his attack. As mentioned in Chapter One, the average criminal is hoping to find an easy victim in "condition white." Imagine his surprise if his potential victim suddenly takes a large lateral step and shouts, "Stay back! Get away from me!" while raising a hand in a stop gesture. Secondly, issuing commands alerts anyone within the immediate vicinity that an attack is underway and that we're the non-aggressor.

When we do issue commands, we need to bark them out in a command voice, deep from the diaphragm. Even the smallest individual can pack a verbal punch when he or she practices commands such as:

"Stay back! Get away from me! Drop your weapon!"

You'll notice that the language we used was non-threatening and identifies us as the victim. Remember that witnesses may repeat everything that you say, so avoid language like this:

"If you come any closer, I'll kill you!"
or, "I'm going to blow your %$@ing head off!"*

Our advice is to work these verbal commands into the mental scenarios discussed in Chapter One, as well as into your range or virtual exercises. Training consistently with this method gives us the confidence that commands and movement will be an automated part of our defense in a critical incident.

What Are Our Options?

So we've found ourselves in the middle of a situation that we didn't start and we couldn't avoid. What should our goal be at this point? Besides the obvious answer of survival, our goal should be to do *anything that affects our attacker's ability to commence an attack.* It's important to remember that in most violent attacks, we have options—finding cover, putting barriers between us and the attacker, or choosing a less–than–lethal level of force such as exposing our firearm or even pointing it at the attacker. *Anything* that causes our attacker to break off his attack before it begins is a good thing. Finally, it's important to realize that our decision to use any level of force will be second-guessed by the police, the prosecutor, and possibly a jury. We'll have to meet the "reasonableness" test, and if a prosecutor believes that we used excessive force, we're going to have to try to convince a jury that we're right, and the prosecutor is wrong.

Escape
Even after a violent attack has commenced, if we can escape, we *should* escape.

Cover and Barriers
We should place *anything* between us and the attacker that can protect us from the attacker's weapon(s) or that can disrupt his attack.

Exposing Our Firearm
There are no guarantees, but most violent crimes end if the victim simply exposes a firearm. Most criminals want to leave the scene of the crime with the same number of holes they started with.

Drawing Our Firearm
It's a big jump up on the "Use of Force" continuum, but drawing our firearm immediately indicates to a determined attacker that we're not going to be an easy victim. Forcefully barking out commands such as "Stop!" also gives him a chance to change his mind before it's too late. Remember that just because you've drawn your firearm does *not* mean that you need to press the trigger.

Using Our Firearm
When we have *no other choice,* we need to be prepared to stop the threat with any force necessary.

WHEN WE'RE LEFT WITH NO OTHER CHOICE

Up to this point in the book, it's fair to say that everything we've discussed has been fairly academic, including the deadly force scenarios that were discussed in Chapter Four. On this page, we're going to need to discuss the most serious topic in the book, namely, shooting at another human being. We truly wish this topic never had to be discussed, but we also wish that criminals didn't murder, rape, assault, and rob. While we'd be the first in line to buy a Star Wars blaster that could be set on stun, we're not lucky enough to have that option. Until that day, if we do find ourselves in a situation that we didn't start and we can't escape from, where all four rules governing the use of deadly force have been met, then we have no choice but to stop the threat with any force necessary.

Where Do We Shoot?

As discussed in Chapter Three on shooting fundamentals, if we must use our firearm, our goal is "defensive accuracy." Defensive accuracy is any round that *significantly affects the attacker's ability to continue his attack*. The illustration to the right is a fair approximation of the human body, internally and externally. Where would you shoot to meet the goal of defensive accuracy? Would you shoot for the arm or shoulder? How about the attacker's hand? If those shots hit, they might affect the attacker's *desire* to continue an attack, but probably not his *ability*. Remember that your attacker will also be under the effects of adrenaline and endorphins, and he'll have a heightened pain threshold. If he's consumed illicit drugs such as Methamphetamine, his pain threshold will be

even higher. It's very possible that he wouldn't even feel a bullet if it passed through one of the areas on the diagram that contains no bone or organs. How about if you missed those small, moving targets? Remember that under the physiological effects that you'll undergo, your accuracy is likely to suffer, and the penalty for a miss can range from lost seconds and one less bullet, to the death of an innocent bystander. Keep in mind that we've moved beyond the academic and we're now talking about what it would take to stop an attacker who is seconds away from (or is already) stabbing you, shooting you, choking you, raping you, or beating you. It's a cold reality, but the fastest, surest, safest way (safest to innocent bystanders, not safest to the attacker) to significantly affect an attacker's ability to continue an attack, is to use the method taught to every police agency in the U.S., which is to aim for the attacker's "cardiovascular triangle." When the cardiovascular triangle isn't visible, police are taught to shoot at the "center of exposed mass," which is the center of the largest part of the attacker's body that's visible.

How Long Do We Shoot?

As tempted as you may be to prematurely end your defense to see what effect your bullets have had, it's important to continue your defense until the attack has ended. It won't be like the movies, where one moderately sized bullet throws the bad guy through a plate glass window—odds are, you won't be able to tell where your bullets impact, or even *if* they have impacted. The only information that you'll be receiving will be whether the attack is continuing or whether it's ended. The moment it ends is the moment you *must stop using deadly force*.

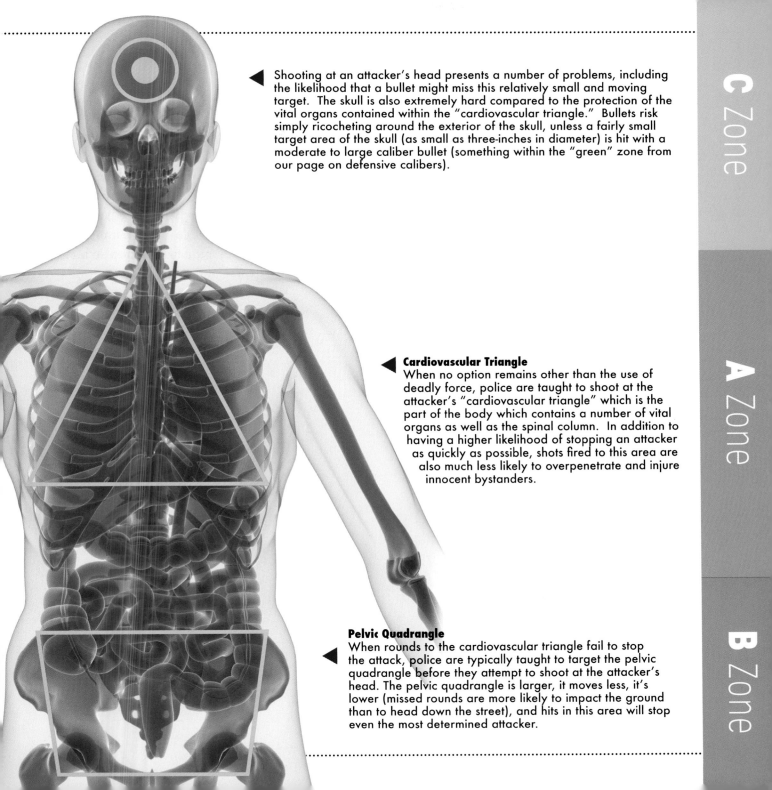

Shooting at an attacker's head presents a number of problems, including the likelihood that a bullet might miss this relatively small and moving target. The skull is also extremely hard compared to the protection of the vital organs contained within the "cardiovascular triangle." Bullets risk simply ricocheting around the exterior of the skull, unless a fairly small target area of the skull (as small as three-inches in diameter) is hit with a moderate to large caliber bullet (something within the "green" zone from our page on defensive calibers).

Cardiovascular Triangle
When no option remains other than the use of deadly force, police are taught to shoot at the attacker's "cardiovascular triangle" which is the part of the body which contains a number of vital organs as well as the spinal column. In addition to having a higher likelihood of stopping an attacker as quickly as possible, shots fired to this area are also much less likely to overpenetrate and injure innocent bystanders.

Pelvic Quadrangle
When rounds to the cardiovascular triangle fail to stop the attack, police are typically taught to target the pelvic quadrangle before they attempt to shoot at the attacker's head. The pelvic quadrangle is larger, it moves less, it's lower (missed rounds are more likely to impact the ground than to head down the street), and hits in this area will stop even the most determined attacker.

AFTER THE THREAT HAS ENDED

Remember that the right to use deadly force ends the moment any one of the rules governing the use of deadly force is no longer true. Some examples of this might include:

» The attacker has given up or he's run away. If he's run away, let him go. Protect yourself and your loved ones, tend to the wounded, and be a good witness.

» The attacker has been wounded and can no longer threaten you with death or great bodily harm.

» An opportunity to retreat safely has suddenly become available, such as after the attacker has been injured or has dropped his weapon.

Any use of force out of anger, retribution, or a misplaced sense of justice is a crime. Once the attack has ended, you can no longer continue to use deadly force, no matter how badly you or another individual might be injured. Picture this horrific scenario— walking through a parking garage, you come upon a rape in progress. You shout a warning and give chase when the attacker flees. You corner him at the end of the parking garage and when he charges you, you shoot and kill him. Your friends and family might call you a "hero," but you may have to hear about it from jail.

» If your attacker ends the attack, your right to use deadly force ends as well. Regardless of how badly injured you or a loved one may be, or how angry you might feel, any harm that comes to the attacker at this point will be on your head. Come to think of it, any harm that came to your attacker before this point will also be on your head. Don't make the situation worse by continuing to shoot after the attack is over.

After you have determined that the threat has ended, visually scan to the left and the right of the initial threat, while keeping your firearm on target. Then lower your firearm to a low ready position (pointed down to the ground in front of you with your finger OUTSIDE of the trigger guard) and perform a 360° scan for other threats. These scans will not only help to identify any other threats, they will also help to break tunnel vision and auditory exclusion (see the box below). Once you've determined that there are no further threats, immediately perform the tasks discussed on the following pages.

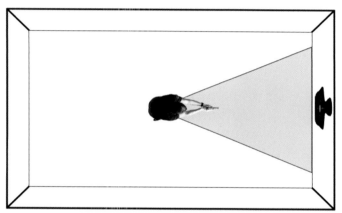

After the threat has ended, scan to the left and right to look for other threats and to break tunnel vision and auditory exclusion.

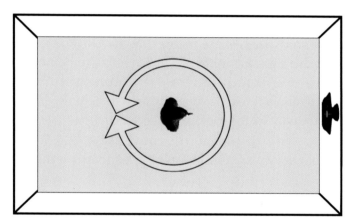

Then lower your firearm to a "low ready" and perform a 360° scan to ensure there are no other threats.

RESETTING THE BRAIN'S FILTERS

» As discussed in the section on the "Physiological Reactions" that typically occur during an attack, you can expect to have tunnel vision and auditory exclusion, which means that you may not see threats beyond the one to your front and you may have diminished hearing. Hunters appreciate auditory exclusion because it means they don't "hear" the shot as it's being fired, but in a defensive situation, auditory exclusion might cause you to ignore a loved one's shouts or the police shouting at you to drop your firearm. Physically moving your head (rather than just moving your eyes) to scan for other threats can break both tunnel vision and auditory exclusion. The brain seems to perceive this scan as a search for new threats and the selective filtering that occurs within the thalamus or sensory cortex is reset to normal.

THE IMMEDIATE AFTERMATH

Once you've confirmed that the immediate threat has ended, you'll need to quickly complete several important tasks. First and foremost, if you believe that you're still in danger, you'll need to immediately retreat to a safe area. Once there, you should closely check yourself and others for any injuries that might be masked by the effects of adrenaline and endorphins, and you should begin emergency first-aid to control any bleeding. Next, you'll need to make several important phone calls, including a call to 911, even if no one (including the attacker) is injured, or even if he's run away. These phone calls are CRITICAL. Even in this stressful moment, you'll need to remember that you've just used a firearm (even if it was just to expose it to end a threat), and you'll need to begin laying the groundwork for your defense in the event that you're charged with a crime. The phone calls to 911 and to your lawyer are the first steps in establishing this.

If you displayed your firearm, but no rounds were fired, make two calls:

1 **Call 911.** Do not let the attacker (or alleged attacker) or witnesses report the incident differently than it happened. This phone call is CRITICAL. Keep the call short and to the point:

A My name is _____ and I need to report (an attack / a possible attack) at (address, intersection, etc.).

B The individual (give a brief description of the attacker) and (ran off / drove off, etc.).

C I do have a permit to carry a firearm, and did expose my firearm to the attacker, but I did not use it.

D I've called my attorney and (he or she) will contact you to schedule time to make a statement. Here is my number.

E Be prepared to answer any questions related to the alleged attacker or your contact information, but do NOT answer any questions about your actions. Be prepared to hang up if the questioning gets persistent.

2 **Call your attorney.** If you can't reach your attorney, leave a message and contact information for where and how he or she can reach you.

If rounds were fired, make three calls:

1 **Call 911.** It is your obligation to seek medical attention if someone is injured! Remember that you are being recorded! Keep your 911 call short and to the point:

> **A** My name is _____ and I need to report an attack at (address, intersection, etc.).

> **B** The attacker (ran away / is injured / needs an ambulance).

> **C** I'm wearing _____ and I do have a permit to carry a firearm so let the police know that I'll place my firearm (on the front seat of my car / on my hood / back in my holster) before they arrive.

> **D** I need to (go help my family / watch the attacker / get to a safer place) so I'm going to hang up now.

> **E** Hang up.

2 **Call your attorney.**

3 **Call your family.** Inform them that you've been involved in a defensive situation and instruct them to speak with no one—not the police, not the media, no one! Tell family members to inform the police that they **DO NOT CONSENT TO A SEARCH OF YOUR HOME OR PROPERTY** and that they will answer no questions unless your attorney is present. If you are calling them from jail, do NOT give them any details, as the call may be recorded. Simply tell them where you are and that they should call your attorney.

When the Police Arrive

When the police arrive on the scene, what's your number one goal? Don't get shot. After a violent confrontation where force may have been used, the police will not know exactly what has occurred. They will only know that a firearm has been used and that the armed person remains at the scene. Remember, the police will be nervous, they'll be concerned for their own safety, and their adrenaline will be flowing as well. They will most likely believe that a bad guy has just shot another bad guy, or a bad guy has just shot a good guy.

Because of the perceptions the police will have when they arrive at the scene, here's what you should do:

» Place your firearm back in its holster or off your body BEFORE the police approach. Where you place it will need to be based upon the current disposition of the attacker. If he's given up and is sitting on the ground in front of you, you'll need to keep ready access to your firearm, so reholstering may be the best idea. If he's run away or is incapacitated, placing the firearm on the hood or top of a car, or on the ground in front of you may be a better idea.

» Put your hands high in the air as the police approach. Don't even *twitch* if your firearm is back in the holster.

» Comply with all instructions from the police and keep your hands where they can see them. This is not the time to explain that "you are the good guy."

» Don't argue, and be prepared to be pushed to the ground, handcuffed, and placed in the back of a squad car.

Digging Yourself a Hole

After a confrontation where a firearm has been used, the police are no longer there to serve and protect you, they are there to serve the prosecutor and protect any case he or she may choose to file. Like they say in the movies, anything you say will be used against you in a court of law. Most police officers carry digital recording devices, which will be rolling the moment they arrive at the scene, and any statement, no matter how innocent (such as "I was mad") can come back to haunt you. Although the police at the scene may legitimately sympathize with you, if the incident results in a trial, the police will be testifying on behalf of the prosecutor, not on your behalf. Finally, it's fair to say that the fatal error of nearly every criminal *and* every responsibly armed citizen involved in an altercation is that they want to talk. In fact, they *love* to talk—to the police, to their family, to the media, and their family even likes to talk to the media. While that may be a natural reaction when you want to shout, "I'm Innocent!" from the rooftops, you must resist that urge during the immediate aftermath of the incident; during intense pressure by the police to make a statement; when walking through a gauntlet of media when leaving jail; or when the media calls the attacker "the victim" and dredges up every questionable incident in your background. You *must* trust your lawyer to get you to the other side intact.

A Four-Part Statement to the Police

There is no upside in speaking with the police without your attorney present, and any statement you make, however true you may believe it to be, is fraught with risk (review our physiological section as a reminder on the distortion that can occur to your memory during an attack). Because of that and other risks, we recommend that you stick with this four-part statement to the police and do NOT go beyond it:

1 I was attacked (by that person / by a person who ran in that direction). Note: If the attacker is no longer present, be very careful about giving a description to the police since you may be suffering from memory loss or false memories, and you may not provide an accurate description.

2 There is the evidence (point out anything that the police may miss or may not realize was used as a weapon).

3 That person / those people were witnesses.

4 I've spoken with / left a message with my attorney and I'm going to wait until (he or she) arrives to give a statement and sign a complaint.

Note: If your mind goes blank, at least remember #4 above and do *not* be embarrassed to read the statement above if you choose to photocopy this page and keep it in your wallet or purse.

» You don't have to be a fan of the CSI television shows to know that the police will carefully document everything they find at the scene of the attack. Don't disturb any evidence, and be sure to point out anything to the police that they might miss, such as the attacker's weapon.

THE MIRANDA WARNING

Most Americans are aware that the Fifth Amendment forbids compelling a person to testify against himself or herself in a criminal trial, and any fan of TV police dramas knows about the Miranda warning which reminds suspects of their right to remain silent, but do you know what Miranda *really* means, and when police are required to provide it?

Is it Enough Just to be Silent?

As part of the 1966 "Miranda" decision (Miranda v. Arizona) and subsequent reinterpretations, the Supreme Court has concluded that it is only necessary for police to read the Miranda warning to suspects upon their actual arrest and formal interrogation (Illinois v. Perkins). Prior to the combination of those two events, no warning is required, and most police departments now train their officers to delay the warning until just prior to the suspect's formal interrogation, which gives the suspect plenty of time to say something incriminating. If at any point the suspect does invoke his or her right to remain silent, it officially ends the police's right to a formal interrogation, but it *doesn't* end their right to use any statement that was voluntarily given, before, or after the Miranda warning.

So we know that we have the *right* to remain silent, but it begs the question, what does it take to *invoke* that right? Is it enough to simply remain silent? The answer is no. In 2010, the Supreme Court decided in Berghuis v. Thompkins, that simply remaining silent wasn't the same thing as explicitly *invoking* your right to remain silent with a clear statement. Without that statement, police have the right to continue their formal or informal interrogation for hours, in the hopes that you'll eventually say something to incriminate yourself. Knowing that, after making the four-part statement to the police shown on the previous page, you should state very clearly:

"I want my lawyer present before I answer any questions, and until then, I invoke my right to remain silent."

Keep in mind that even if you've been given your Miranda warning, and even if you've explicitly invoked your right to remain silent, anything that you volunteer (what's called a "spontaneous statement") is admissible in court. In other words, it isn't enough just to invoke your right to remain silent; after that, you'll have to actually *be* silent.

> " *I want my lawyer present before I answer any questions, and until then, I invoke my right to remain silent.* "

When Asked if you Consent to a Search

When asked if you consent to a search of your person, your vehicle, or your home, state very clearly:

"I do not consent to a search of my person or my property."

Repeat as often as necessary. Experts have agreed that there is zero upside in agreeing to a search. That said, do not interfere with the police if they choose to go ahead with a search anyway, without your consent. Police will frame their question to you in a way that makes it sound as though it's a foregone conclusion—for example, they won't ask, "Do you give up your rights under the Fourth Amendment of the constitution?" Instead they'll say, "It's okay if we look through your car, right?" Your answer needs to be "No." The problem with consenting to a search isn't just what will happen if the police find something illegal. In the hands of the prosecutor, even legal items can taint a jury. For example, a box of ammunition found in your home or car becomes, "The defendant had enough ammunition to kill 50 people!" That pain pill found under your front seat that was prescribed to you three years ago becomes, "The defendant was found with illegal prescription drugs!" As our friend Marc Berris says, "The laws protecting us from illegal search and seizure are designed to protect the innocent, not the guilty."

When are you Under Arrest?

Unfortunately, it won't be as obvious as when Horatio Cane says, "Take him!" on CSI Miami. When investigating any suspicious activity (which would include the use of a firearm) the police have the right to perform what is referred to as a Terry stop, which allows the police to temporarily detain individuals to request that they identify themselves; to question them about the suspicious activity; and to conduct a limited pat down search for weapons. Whether you've moved from a Terry stop to being under arrest may only be ascertained if you are not allowed to leave. To determine that, after you've made the four-part statement, you'll need to ask, "Can I leave?" If the answer is no, you should assume that you're under arrest.

Advice for your Lawyer

When discussing your case with your lawyer, here are a few extra bits of information that you should pass on. If they don't understand the points below, or are unwilling to complete these tasks, find a new lawyer.

» Delay any interview with the police for as long as possible, but for at least 48-hours. Refer your lawyer to the International Association of Chiefs of Police (IACP) guidelines shown on the next page, that the police themselves will follow if they are involved in a critical incident.

❝ I do not consent to a search of my person or my property. ❞

» Your lawyer should read the physiological section in this book so he or she can understand the distortions that occur during critical incidents. He or she should also review the police interviews by Dr. Alexis Artwohl.

» Your lawyer and his or her investigator must review the scene of the crime, they must analyze all evidence, and they must conduct their own interviews of all witnesses.

» Your lawyer may need to seek out expert testimony from professionals who have testified at (and won) multiple self-defense trials.

How are Police Treated when a Shooting Occurs?

Most law enforcement organizations in the U.S. have adopted policies similar to one outlined by the International Association of Chiefs of Police, which provides 20 guidelines for dealing with a police officer who has been involved in a shooting. These guidelines are designed to have the officers avoid a "second injury" by insensitive treatment and to allow the officer to "avoid legal complications."

One of the guidelines states: "If possible, the officer can benefit from some recovery time before detailed interviewing begins. This can range from a few hours to overnight, depending on the emotional state of the officer and the circumstances." It goes on to say, "Officers who have been afforded this opportunity to calm down are likely to provide a more coherent and accurate statement."

If that advice is good enough for the police, it's good enough for us.

>> In the euphoria of the aftermath, you might think that the situation is a slam dunk in your favor and that you'll be hailed as a hero. We hate to burst your bubble, but it isn't, and you won't. When you run through the mental scenarios in Chapter One, don't forget to include your arrest.

CHAPTER 6

GEAR AND GADGETS

» EXPLAINING HOLSTER RETENTION

» TYPES OF HOLSTERS INCLUDING BELT, PANCAKE, INSIDE THE WAISTBAND, AND HOLSTERS FOR DEEP CONCEALMENT

» OTHER GEAR INCLUDING BELTS, TACTICAL FLASHLIGHTS, MOUNTED LIGHTS, NIGHT SIGHTS, AND LASERS

» GUN SAFES AND STORAGE

Walk into any gun shop, and the variety of gear and gadgets available can be a bit overwhelming. Gun vaults, holsters, lights, lasers—where do you start? In this chapter, we'll help to explain each of those pieces of related gear, and we'll talk about the options you should consider when you're ready to go shopping. Some of the gear we'll discuss such as gun vaults, lights, and lasers, will be beneficial regardless of whether you're looking at home defense or if a concealed carry permit is part of your plan. If you *are* considering a concealed carry permit, then your immediate priority will need to be a good holster that not only works for your firearm, but that also works for *you*. Since selecting a holster can be as confusing as selecting a firearm, we're going to start with that topic.

In our section on holsters, we'll start by explaining how holster retention devices work (and which levels of retention work for permit holders, versus what law enforcement might require) as well as explanations of the most common types of holsters, including belt, pancake, paddle, pocket, and others. In our examples, you'll see a number of holsters made with leather and a number made with Kydex, which is a fancy way of saying plastic. Both have advantages—leather can be more comfortable and is usually more kind to your handgun's finish, while Kydex typically has much more of a positive "click" when the firearm is holstered. We have lots of each.

We'll continue the chapter with discussions on other important pieces of equipment, including gear to allow you to operate in low-light or no-light situations. Night sights, tactical flashlights, mounted lights, and mounted lasers have all undergone a dramatic transformation in the last decade, and we'll provide a detailed explanation about what you should consider when selecting these pieces of equipment.

Finally, we'll wrap-up this chapter with a discussion of safe storage devices for your home, including gun vaults designed to hold a single handgun (along with a spare magazine or two), and wall mounted units designed to secure home defense shotguns.

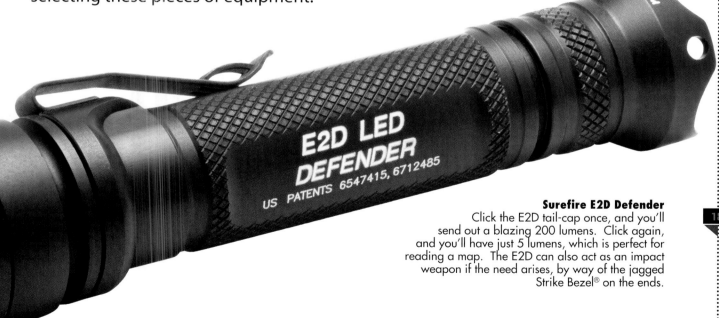

Surefire E2D Defender
Click the E2D tail-cap once, and you'll send out a blazing 200 lumens. Click again, and you'll have just 5 lumens, which is perfect for reading a map. The E2D can also act as an impact weapon if the need arises, by way of the jagged Strike Bezel® on the ends.

LEVELS OF HOLSTER RETENTION

Modern holsters come with a variety of methods and devices to ensure that your handgun remains in the holster until you're ready to use it. The most common retention method that holsters provide is nothing more than a snug fit. Selecting a holster that's molded to your specific firearm make, model, and size usually means that the firearm will remain in place even when you're running, jumping, or bending, but it allows your firearm to be quickly retrieved without an extra step, something you'll appreciate during an attack when your manual dexterity can go to mush. These holsters are typically referred to as "Level Zero" or "Open Top Holsters." For an extra level of retention, a variety of holsters are available with top straps, or some type of release lever, usually activated with either the index finger or with the thumb. These holsters are typically referred to as "Level I" holsters, and can provide an extra level of confidence that your gun will remain in the holster until you need it.

LEVEL ZERO: Firearm Held in Place by Tension only

Retention by Tension
Both leather and plastic Level Zero holsters hold firearms in place by being specifically molded to a particular firearm.

Tension Screws
Some Level Zero holsters may add a tension screw or two that allows the holster's retention to be tightened or loosened.

LEVEL I: Firearm Held in Place by Top Strap or Release Lever

Top Strap
Usually unsnapped by pushing the thumb toward the body while drawing.

Release Lever
A release lever is embedded within the holster and is released with either the index or middle finger. A solid "click" should be heard when reholstering.

So What are Level II and Level III holsters?

Law enforcement officers are often required by their departments to use what are called Level II or Level III holsters, which have multiple retention methods that must be de-activated before the firearm can be drawn from the holster. Our advice is that you leave these holsters to the police. Since police typically carry exposed and have the unfortunate task of getting their hands on bad guys, the extra retention makes sense.

1 **Top Strap**
Usually unsnapped by pushing the thumb toward the body while drawing. Others, such as this Safariland holster, have straps that must be rotated forward before the firearm can be released.

2 **Release Lever**
A release lever is embedded within the holster and is released with either the index or middle finger.

3 **Rocking Release**
Once the top strap is released and the release lever is pushed, the firearm can only be drawn after rocking it back (or forward, depending upon the brand).

HIP HOLSTERS

Hip holsters are designed to be worn on the belt, outside of the waistband. "Belt loop" holsters are usually attached by a single loop behind the holster, while "pancake holsters" typically have two widely-spaced slots, allowing them to be held very tightly to the body for extra concealment. Most pancake holsters are designed to be worn on the strong side, but several (such as the "Cross Guard" from Side Guard Holsters) are designed to be worn on the weak side with a cross draw cant. Each style has pros and cons. Belt holsters can sometimes ride too far from the body, while some leather pancake holsters can occasionally fit too close to the body, causing them to collapse when the firearm is drawn, requiring two hands to re-holster.

Pancake holsters such as the Reflex Holster from Uncle Mike's, typically have two belt slots, which hold the holster and firearm closer to the body for better control and concealment.

Belt loop holsters such as this holster from Blade-Tech, typically have a single loop in the back that the belt is threaded through. Blade-Tech offers this innovative clip that can be unsnapped and threaded through the belt, then re-snapped without removing the belt.

Blade-Tech WRS Duty Holster with TEK-LOK (Back View)

PADDLE HOLSTERS

Paddle holsters are so easy to attach and remove that they can offer some incentive to carry when you might rather not take the time to remove your belt to attach a through-the-belt holster. Find one that has a secure "tooth" that will bite into your pants, below your belt. This will ensure that the holster remains firmly attached to your belt after you draw the handgun, rather than becoming detached with the handgun still tightly holstered (which would be dangerous and really, really embarrassing). Paddle holsters do tend to stand farther away from the body than belt or pancake holsters, which can be a plus if you prefer not to feel the holster, but a negative if you are carrying a heavier pistol (which can flop around) or are looking to conceal the outline of your firearm.

Uncle Mike's Reflex Paddle Holster
This model from Uncle Mike's allows the user to adjust the "drop" of the firearm (how high or low it is on the belt) by changing the location of where the paddle is mounted to the holster pocket. In addition, with the quick change of a few screws, the holster can also be converted into the pancake holster shown on the opposite page, using the pancake holster attachment, which is included.

POCKET HOLSTERS

Pocket Pistols are small enough for alternate carry options, including sliding them into the front or back pocket. The holster on the right is designed to be carried in the front pocket—that additional piece of leather under the grips is designed to hook on your pocket while drawing, leaving the holster in your pocket and the gun in your hand. The holster on the far right is designed for the back pocket. The solid piece of leather behind the gun faces the outside of the pants, breaking up the outline of the gun.

INSIDE THE WAISTBAND HOLSTERS

Like they sound, inside the waistband holsters are tucked inside the pants, usually secured to the belt with a loop or hook system. IWB holsters are appropriate when deeper concealment is desired, and it allows the holster to be concealed even when a golf shirt or t-shirt is worn, rather than a longer outer garment. We recommend that if you decide on an IWB holster, you select one that's rigid and molded for your specific firearm of choice. This ensures that the holster doesn't collapse after drawing, allowing you to re-holster using a single hand. The inside the waistband holster shown here has an innovative feature allowing the shirt to be tucked in between the holster and clip.

Side Guard Holsters "Rough Out"   **Side Guard Holsters "Rough Wallet"**

Side Guard Holsters "Tuck Clip"

ANKLE HOLSTERS

Ankle holsters don't provide the easiest method to draw from, but they can offer deep concealment when the situation calls for it. Our suggestion is to stick with pocket-sized pistols for ankle carry, otherwise you'll feel like you strapped on an ankle weight.

Galco Ankle Glove

FANNY PACK HOLSTERS

Galco Elite

Fanny pack holsters allow the firearm to be carried in an easily accessible location, without giving away the fact that you happen to be carrying. Next time you see someone wearing a fanny pack, look to see if his wallet is in his back pocket. If it is, it's a good bet that he's carrying a gun in the pack. On the other hand, if you can't see a wallet and he's also wearing Zubaz, then there's a good chance he's just stuck in the '80s.

HOLSTERS FOR THE CAR

DeSantis Kingston Car Seat Holster

The seatbelt has a habit of lying in a perfect position to block access to your firearm when using a hip holster. So when carrying in your vehicle, a better option might be to invest in a holster designed for automobile carry, like the DeSantis Kingston holster (we have one and love it). Like the other "off the body" holsters, you must ensure that your firearm *never* leaves your immediate control.

PURSE HOLSTERS

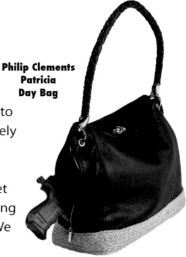

Philip Clements Patricia Day Bag

Purse holsters have a dedicated pocket designed to hold a handgun more securely and covertly than simply dropping it into a normal purse. This dedicated pocket however, should carry nothing else besides the handgun. We were tempted to put purse holsters on our "not recommended" list, since a purse is the most likely object to be grabbed during a robbery, but we realize that a purse holster might be the best option for certain individuals. To avoid the "grab" problem, always loop the purse around your neck, and *never* allow it to leave your direct control.

SHOULDER HOLSTERS

Pretty cool if your name is Crocket or Tubbs, but somewhat impractical otherwise. If concealment is desired or required, shoulder holsters will require that an outer garment be worn, and they tend to be more difficult to draw from versus holsters worn on the belt. One exception is for individuals of sizable girth (who are less comfortable with a belt or IWB holster); another is for individuals who spend most of their time in a vehicle, since a shoulder holster won't be blocked by the seatbelt.

DON'T FORGET THE BELT

Typical dress belts are not nearly stiff enough (and are rarely wide enough) to support the weight of a firearm, however, a number of manufacturers (including 5.11, Gould & Goodrich, Galco, and Bianchi) offer dress, casual, and tactical versions specifically designed to support the weight of a gun. If fitting to a belt holster, ensure that the width of the belt matches the belt loop slots in the holster. A proper belt can also make a common function a little bit easier and a little bit safer. Using the restroom while holstered presents challenges, so we recommend that you invest in a very rigid belt so that your holstered firearm doesn't drop to the floor, or you can un-holster and put the firearm in your pocket. If your belt is long enough, you can re-fasten your belt with your pants in the lowered position. DO NOT set your firearm on the floor, or hang your firearm on the coat hook on the stall door. That leaves it in a perfect position to be forgotten or grabbed while you're busy doing other things, and it can lead to a negligent discharge, and a lot of embarrassment.

TACTICAL FLASHLIGHTS

When preparing your gear selections for home defense or concealed carry, we'd recommend that you include a tactical flashlight on your short list of things to purchase. The term "tactical flashlight" is more than just marketing—there are major differences between flashlights that should be part of your self-defense line-up, versus what you'd pick up at your local hardware store for $10. Here's what you should look for in a tactical flashlight:

High Output Beam. A minimum brightness should be 60 lumens (the average 2-AA light is about 15 lumens). 60 lumens is bright enough to momentarily blind an attacker even in daylight, while 125 lumens is like staring into the sun. Surefire has lights up to 900 lumens, such as the M3LT-S CombatLight shown below. Personally, we'd rather be Tasered than have one of those hit us in the face.

Lithium Batteries, which have a shelf-life as long as ten years, and have a much higher energy output for their size, versus alkaline batteries. In addition, they aren't affected by cold, so feel free to leave the light in your car, even in the northern states.

Tail-Cap On/Off Switch, rather than a switch on the side. As you'll see in our section on the various flashlight holds in Chapter Seven, a tail-cap on/off switch is critical to getting these holds correct.

We'd also recommend LED lights over traditional tungsten bulbs. You can hammer nails with an LED light without it breaking, while tungsten bulbs can break if the flashlight is dropped or banged on a barrier.

Handheld Lights

A number of manufacturers make handheld flashlights that fit these criteria, including the lights shown here from Surefire and First-Light USA. While it might seem like a simple thing to fire a gun while simultaneously holding a flashlight, it's going to take some practice, so we've provided a number of photos, and a range exercise in Chapter Seven for you to follow.

Surefire M3LT-S Combat Light
The new M3LT-S from Surefire isn't a flashlight you'd use to light up a map on a late night hike unless you want to light it on fire (metaphorically speaking of course). At 900 lumens, the M3LT-S won't just momentarily blind an attacker, it will bring him to his knees.

Surefire 6PX Defender

The new 6PX from Surefire puts out a blinding 200 lumens of power, with a runtime of about two hours. Like the E2D profiled in the chapter introduction, the 6PX also had a strike bezel, which can act as an impact weapon when required.

Surefire Z2S Combat Light

The new Z2S from Surefire puts out 160 lumens, more than enough power to light up a scene or blind an attacker. The Z2S also has rubber rings around the center, which allows you to use the Rogers/Surefire flashlight hold, which we'll explain in Chapter Seven.

First Light Liberator

The Liberator by First-Light, is a unique design that offers a great compromise between handheld and mounted flashlights. The Liberator's handle loops through the support hand and allows a proper grip on the firearm (and also allows magazines to be changed and malfunctions to be cleared without dropping the light). It also allows the user to scan the area independent of the direction that the muzzle is pointed, something not available with mounted lights. The Liberator ST is a blazing 120 lumens and is thumb activated with three switches on the support bar (momentary, strobe, or constant).

» Whether operating with a handgun, a shotgun, an AR-15, or no firearm at all, a good tactical flashlight will not only chase away the shadows, it might also chase away the bad guy with no shots fired.

Mounted Lights

In addition to selecting a good handheld tactical flashlight, we'd also recommend that you consider a mounted light, whether that light is mounted to your handgun, your home defense shotgun, or your AR-15. When using a mounted light, it's important to remember that when we point the *light*, we're also pointing our *muzzle*, so we need to consider the light part of our firearm system, and not a separate light that should be used to peek into corners. Our three favorite mounted lights are from Surefire, and are shown here.

Surefire Forend Mounted Light for Shotguns

Surefire makes replacement forends for Benelli, FN, Mossberg, Remington, and Winchester shotguns. Turning them on or off is done by depressing the momentary pressure pad on the opposite side, or the constant on/off rocker switch shown here.

Surefire X400 Light/Laser for Semi-Automatic Handguns

The Surefire X400 combines an incredibly bright light at 170 lumens with a bright red laser into a single package. With the switch shown at the back, the user can switch between momentary or constant operation for the light only, the laser only, or both simultaneously.

Surefire M900V Pistol Grip Mounted Light for AR-15s

With an output of 150 lumens, the M900V pistol grip light is perfect for lighting up a hallway if a bad guy is heading toward you and your family. The pressure pads visible on the side of the M900V allow you to momentarily light up a scene, while the dial on the bottom allows you to turn to constant on, or disable the light. Additionally, the M900V comes with an additional pressure pad at the back of the light (about where the thumb would fall), which provides a low output LED light, which is enough light to navigate by, but not enough so that an attacker can identify your location.

LASER SIGHTS

Ask any group of seasoned shooters, and odds are, they might just roll their eyes when you ask about using laser sights on your firearm. In response, you may want to quote a Crimson Trace advertisement: "Don't let your ego obscure your target, because as good as you are with a gun, a laser sight makes you better." Crimson Trace might just have a point. Looking at a summary of shootings by the New York Police Department in 2005, two things jump out. The first is that 72 percent of the reported shootings occurred between dusk and dawn. That high percentage of shootings in low light situations calls into question a training regimen that relies solely on the traditional method of "indexing" on a target by aligning the front and rear sights. The second surprising statistic from the NYPD shootings was that the accuracy of the involved officers was well below what would have been expected, since most officers train frequently with their firearms. To paraphrase Crimson Trace, something is turning these officers from 90 percenters on the range, to 5—50 percenters in the field. Is it because of the extreme stress? Is it the low light? Is it a lack of realism in the officer's training program?

We'll address the last topic in Chapter Seven, but let's hit those first two issues here. As discussed in Chapter Five, we know that our higher brain is going to check out during periods of extreme stress and that automated responses will take over to one degree or another. So if there's a complex way of doing things and a simple way of doing things, we need to pick simple. If there's a method that embraces those natural responses or fights them, we need to embrace them. Let's take sight alignment as an example. A traditional sight plane requires that three objects be aligned—the rear sight, the front sight, and the target. In addition, it fights the mind's natural inclination to focus on the threat, and forces us to change our focus to the front sight.

Point shooting takes a massive step in the right direction by reducing the indexes from three down to just one (the target) and it embraces our natural instinct to focus on the target, but the "margin of error" might be greater than we can allow. Point shooting also relies on an ability to make the firearm an extension of our arms; that is, we need to know where the firearm is pointing, which requires the arms to be extended as far as possible. When we're unable to use that proper arm extension—for example, when rapidly retreating, when prone, after being knocked over, or with our firearm in a tight retention position (drawn back to our side, rather than extended out straight), the margin of error can be dramatically increased. Like point shooting, using a laser simplifies the traditional sight picture from three indexes down to one, and it allows us to embrace our body's natural

NYPD Accuracy by Distance

Source: NYPD 2005 Firearms Discharge Report

DISTANCE	SHOTS	HITS	HIT PERCENT
0 – 2 Yards	127	65	51%
3 – 7 Yards	155	68	44%
8 – 15 Yards	205	14	7%
16 – 25 Yards	93	5	5%
Total	580	152	26%

» Crimson Trace is arguably the leader in laser sights,
with grip and rail sights developed for nearly every
make and model of handgun, rifle and shotgun.

reaction to focus on the threat. The edge that a laser provides is that it allows us to become indexed on the target much more rapidly, and with a much smaller margin of error. While there's no such thing as laser guided bullets, it's fair to say that if we've followed just two of the building blocks of shooting fundamentals (a solid grip and proper trigger press) our margin of error can be dramatically reduced, even when shooting from those awkward positions described earlier. A laser also allows us to combine indexing strategies. If we've trained using the point/intuitive shooting method, then we've already trained ourselves to elevate the firearm into our sight plane. We can then transition from unsighted fire, to focusing on the red dot, to focusing on the front sight.

Why Train with Anything Else?

It's possible to draw the conclusion that since the physiological reactions that we'll experience will force us to look at the threat rather than the sights, why train with anything but a laser? There are several reasons. First, like all technologies, lasers can fail and batteries can run out. Second, there are environments that are inhospitable to lasers, such as bright light situations, situations where the attacker is wearing a red shirt, or a situation where more than one defender is using a laser on the same threat (that is, how do you know which red dot is yours?) Combining training and technology is a better way to use the laser as a tool, without becoming dependant.

Combining Training and Technology

Used properly, lasers can actually help us to become more proficient at point/intuitive shooting *and* sighted fire. It can even help us to improve our trigger control. Here's how:

Point/Intuitive Shooting. Using a side mounted laser (such as the one from Crimson Trace shown here) start from a low ready or high ready position, with your index finger blocking the laser. Fully extend your arms (elevating the firearm up into your sight plane) and point at the center of the target. Once indexed on the target, move your finger to identify where the firearm's barrel is actually pointing. This method will help you identify when your arms are too high, too low, etc., and, it can help you determine if your pistol's natural point of aim is right for *you*. Repeating this drill dozens of times per day will begin to build in the proper pathways into the cerebellum, all without a shot being fired.

Sight Alignment. For new shooters who are having difficulty grasping the idea of sight alignment, the use of a laser can help them understand exactly what it means to align the front sight, rear sight, and target. Using a handgun with a laser which has been calibrated to align with the sights at a target 21 feet away, start from a low ready, and then extend your arms, bringing the firearm up into your sight plane. Concentrate on the position of the laser dot, and slowly move your focus to the front sight. Place the red dot on top of the front sight, and then slowly adjust the firearm until the front sight is centered between the rear sight. Many new shooters will have an "Ah ha!" moment using this simple technique.

Trigger Control. During a traditional dry firing exercise, pay close attention to what happens to the red dot prior to and immediately after the hammer/striker falls. If the red dot dances up, down, or off the target, you should revisit the topics on proper grip and trigger press. Check out Chapter Seven for an additional laser based exercise.

» Although most lasers sights on the market are traditional red lasers, Viridian has focused on green lasers, which are considerably more visible than red lasers under a variety of conditions, since the color green is closer to the central spectrum of color visible to the human eye. In particular, in daylight conditions, green lasers can appear as much as fifty times brighter than a red laser. Viridian lasers are rail mounted, and use a custom "draw detection" method to automatically illuminate the laser when the handgun is drawn from a Viridian TacLoc holster.

GUN SAFES AND STORAGE

Any gun shop or sporting goods store will have multiple options for firearms storage, including options for completely enclosing a loaded handgun, or completely enclosing the trigger and trigger guard on a loaded shotgun. Our favorite handgun vaults are biometrically operated (you'll pay extra for that option though) or electronically operated vaults which are opened by placing your fingers into finger impressions, and pressing the keypads in the appropriate sequence. If you're interested in mounting a home defense shotgun to a closet wall, we'd recommend investing in the Solo-Vault from Shotlock described below.

Gunvault SpeedVault

For securing a handgun at home or at the office, the new Speedvault from Gunvault is at the top of our list. Unlike traditional handgun vaults, the Speedvault is designed to drop open in a perfect position to get a proper grip on the handgun, for those times when you need access to your handgun *right now*. The Speedvault is available in either a biometric model or with a more traditional keypad as shown here. Both versions come with back-up cylinder lock.

Shotlock Solo-Vault

The Solo-Vault from Shotlock is a wall mountable shotgun vault, and is designed to completely enclose the shotgun's trigger guard, something not available with other wall mounted units. Opened by pushing the proper sequence of the five push-buttons, the Solo-Vault is designed to keep your shotgun out of the hands of unauthorized individuals, but allows quick access when you need your shotgun *right now*. The innovative Solo-Vault is designed to fit almost any style of shotgun including pump, semi-auto, side-by-side, over-under, and most shotguns with pistol grips.

> CHAPTER 7

BASIC AND ADVANCED SKILLS

In Chapter Three, we introduced you to the building blocks of defensive shooting fundamentals. Of course, it's fair to say that simply reading about those skills from *any* book won't do a thing for you; it's repeated and consistent practice that will build those skills into your neural pathways. The variety of exercises in this chapter are designed to help you gain the competence and consistency that we mentioned in the introduction to Chapter Three. Once you've developed competence and consistency with the basics, the next major challenge is to advance your accuracy and speed, which will constantly be in balance. Many of the exercises in this chapter will work toward speed, others toward accuracy, and some will work toward a balance of both, including three of our personal favorites called the "SEB Drill," the "Colored Number Drill," and the "Push Your Limit Drill," which were developed by Rob Pincus and his staff at I.C.E. Training Company. While most of these exercises can be accomplished through self-led training, others require the guidance of an instructor or the assistance of a friend.

Speaking of building those neural pathways, we've started this chapter by revisiting the topic of "muscle memory," where we'll discuss some of the key items that should be a part of your training regimen, including dry firing, fundamental drills, speed and accuracy drills, and even virtual training. We'll also introduce you to the concepts of drawing from the holster, low light shooting techniques, and the use of lasers, but keep in mind that this chapter is an *introduction* to these topics. If you'd like to dramatically increase your skill sets in speed and accuracy, drawing from the holster, low light shooting, and other advanced techniques, you'll need to spend the time and money to attend one of the advanced shooting schools. On that note, we should

» While dry firing and drawing from the holster with a cleared firearm are great methods to keep those neural pathways strong, there's nothing like a trip to the range to work on the fundamentals, and the speed and accuracy drills outlined in this chapter. The range can also be a classroom, as demonstrated in this photo (taken with a remote camera) at the Gander Mtn. Academy indoor range in Lakeville, Minnesota.

Virtual Training

While dry firing, the fundamental drills, and the speed and accuracy drills can build an incredible skill set in shooters who are willing to dedicate the time, we're still lacking a couple of fundamental training elements when we conduct those exercises on a typical indoor or outdoor range. The problem is twofold: first, while we might run a *mental* exercise in our heads about a paper target actually being a bad guy, the paper target isn't actually shooting back or charging us with a knife. Second, our targets on a typical range are usually restricted to a narrow window of 30—45 degrees to our front. That shortcoming can build the wrong "muscle memory" when it comes to situational awareness. In other words, when shooters *know* that the only targets they'll need to engage are to their front (regardless of whether or not they're practicing a "scan" after the shots are fired), they'll build that narrow focus into their neural pathways which can result in self-inflicted tunnel vision during an actual violent attack. So how do we condition ourselves for threats that are actually shooting back, and for threats that can come from all sides? Until recently, the answer was that there wasn't much you could do about it. That all changed when Gander Mountain launched Gander Mtn. Academy, using technology that was previously available only to elite military and law enforcement units.

Virtual training, or training using laser modified guns and projected images, used to be limited to grainy videos on small screens, and "guns" that didn't come close to simulating the real thing. That's all changed. In addition to the live-fire ranges shown on the previous page, Gander Mtn. Academy also provides virtual target ranges (allowing students to gain confidence with the fundamentals before stepping up to a live firearm), and both 180-degree and 300-degree virtual simulators, using high-definition video, and wrap-around screens that literally immerse you in the action. This immersion environment forces shooters to maintain up to a 360-degree awareness of their surroundings, engaging threats to the front, sides, and even the rear. And of course, unlike traditional paper targets, the "simulated" threats can shoot back, so it's possible to *lose* during a scenario, just as it is in real life. As explained by Gander Mountain Academy, dozens of scenarios are available, all designed to "replicate and prepare you for self-defense situations that you may face in real life." Multiple decision points exist within each scenario, allowing a variety of outcomes based upon your decisions. Gander Mountain Academy also keeps the fun factor high, with their new "Number One Gun" simulation, which allows shooters to compete with each other on a wide variety of scored scenarios, all shown in ultra-high definition. There really isn't anything else like it in the world.

» One shortcoming of typical range drills is that shooters may build the wrong "muscle memory" when it comes to situational awareness. In other words, when shooters know that the only targets they'll need to engage are to their front (regardless of whether or not they're practicing a "scan" after the shots are fired), they'll build that knowledge into their neural pathways, which can result in self-inflicted "tunnel vision" during an actual violent attack. Virtual training on the other hand, like the training available at Gander Mtn. Academy, forces shooters to maintain a 360-degree awareness of their surroundings. The student shown here is operating on Gander Mtn. Academy's 300-degree, high-definition range, where threats can approach from the front, the sides, and yes, even the rear.

Skill Level

BEGINNER

Instructor-Led

Target: Official USPSA / IPSC Target

THE "TEN-TO-THE-ONE" DRILL

Description: We learned this drill from instructor Lou Ann Hamblin at the 2011 IALEFI Master Instructor Development Course in Cortland, New York. The drill is designed to allow shooters to gain a perfect understanding of exactly where their trigger's "break point" is, and to apply a smooth trigger press from start to finish. Starting from a shooting stance, the shooter will slowly press the trigger while their assistant counts down from ten to one. When the assistant reaches "one," the student should have reached the trigger's break point, and the gun should fire—not before, and not after. After warming up, the assistant will speed up the drill with the commands, "Ten-to-the-five, four, three, two, one!"

Goal: Many shooters begin their trigger press smoothly, and then "jerk" the trigger in the final stages of the trigger press, which will cause the shot to pull in the direction of the shooting hand. This exercise is designed to force an intense concentration on learning exactly where a pistol's break point is, and to keep the trigger press slow and smooth from the trigger's rest position to the break point where the pistol will fire, without jerking the trigger.

Distance: 21 Feet

Things That a Coach Can Watch For: Listen for shots before or after the assistant reaches a count of one.

Alternatives: Occasionally reverse the count, so that the shooter must release pressure on the trigger, such as "Ten-to-the-five, four, three, two, three, four, five, four, three, two, one!"

THE "SHOOT SMALL/ MISS SMALL" DRILL

Description: The "Shoot Small/Miss Small" drill is one of our favorites, that we first learned from our friends at Bill's Gun Shop & Range in Robbinsdale, MN. Starting from the low or high ready position, the shooter will fire a single round at the back of a USPSA / IPSC target (or any piece of cardboard) then fire strings of two to five rounds at the hole she just made.

Goal: This exercise is designed to force an intense concentration on accuracy by making the "target" no larger than a bullet hole. Many shooters will allow their degree of "slop" to be dictated by how large their target is, so the "Shoot Small/Miss Small" drill is designed to force extra attention on precision.

Distance: 7—14 Feet

Things That a Coach Can Watch For: Watch for the shooter attempting to use the same speed she uses for much larger target areas or for relying only on sight shooting to be extra precise. With plenty of practice (and these distances), the average shooter can become very accurate using point/instinctive shooting, even with a target as small as 22/100ths of an inch.

Skill Level

BEGINNER

Self-Led

Target: Back of an Official USPSA / IPSC Target

DRAWING FROM THE HOLSTER

1 A safe draw from the holster uses a four step draw (performed smoothly) combined with the lessons learned from the four Universal Safety Rules. Step number one is to gain a solid grip on the firearm with the web of the hand high on the backstrap, as it would be once all fundamentals are established. (You should not need to adjust your grip once you've completed your draw.) The trigger finger should be straight and extended along the side of the holster. The support hand should be brought into the body to ensure that it does NOT cross the muzzle during the draw.

2 The firearm should be lifted straight up to ensure that it properly clears the holster, and immediately rotated forward smoothly in the direction of the target or attacker. The support hand should remain in close to the body until the firearm begins its forward motion so that the muzzle cannot cross the support hand. At that point, the support hand can move away from the body to meet the strong hand.

3 The support hand locks in with a proper grip with the fingers butted up against the bottom of the trigger guard. The now complete two-handed grip should not require adjustment once on target. Since we've already rotated the firearm toward the target once the firearm cleared the holster, we should now be transitioning through a high ready position.

4 The arms are punched out from the high ready, with the firearm elevated into the shooter's line of sight.

≫ Rob Pincus is the owner of I.C.E. Training Company and the Developer of the Combat Focus® Shooting Program. Rob leads a team of certified instructors who train thousands of responsibly armed Americans, military personal, law enforcement officers, and security professionals annually. Rob has written and taught extensively on the topic of firearms and tactical training for over a decade, and is one of the busiest professional instructors in the industry.

THE "SEB" DRILL

Description: One of our favorite speed and accuracy drills, taught to us by Rob Pincus from I.C.E. Training Company. Starting from the holster, or from the low or high ready position, the shooter will fire on command of an assistant. The assistant will vary the commands between calls of "Up!" and one of the numbers (such as "Two!") On a call of "Up" the shooter will fire at the large square in the high center of the silhouette, and on the command of a number, the shooter will fire at the appropriately-numbered shape surrounding the large silhouette. The assistant can choose to call more commands of "Up" or more commands of the numbered shapes, in order to vary the shooter's need to balance speed with accuracy.

Goal: This exercise will force the shooter to vary his balance of speed and accuracy on the same target and within the same exercise.

Distance: 7—14 Feet

Things That a Coach Can Watch For: Watch for the shooter attempting to shoot the smaller, numbered targets with the same speed that he uses to shoot the larger square in the silhouette. If he is consistently missing the smaller targets, he'll need to slow those shots down. On the other hand, if he's shooting with a consistent speed for the large and small targets and consistently hitting each target, he can afford to speed up his shots on the larger square.

Skill Level

INTERMEDIATE

Instructor-Led

Target: SEB Training Target

Skill Level

INTERMEDIATE

Instructor-Led

Target: Law Enforcement Target Co.'s
DT-2C Target

THE "COLORED NUMBERS" DRILL

Description: Another great one from Rob Pincus. Starting from the holster, or from the low or high ready position, the shooter will fire on command of an assistant. At stage one, the assistant will call four of the six colored numbers, an equal number of times. The distance to the target will then be doubled and stage two will be fired with the assistant calling the two remaining colored targets.

Goal: This exercise allows the shooter to understand how distance affects his "personal balance of speed and precision." The shooter's goal should be to maintain 100% defensive accuracy (what Rob calls "Combat Accuracy") with no shots off the colored numbers.

Distance:
Stage One: 6—8 Feet
Stage Two: 12—16 Feet

Things That a Coach Can Watch For: As with all exercises, watch for "fast misses," indicating that the shooter needs to slow down; or overly tight groups, indicating that the shooter can speed up.

THE "PUSH YOUR LIMIT" DRILL

Description: The "Push Your Limit" drill was introduced to Rob Pincus by Brad Schuppan and is used to force students to shoot at a progressively faster pace until they eventually move beyond their own personal balance of speed and accuracy.

Stage One: The shooter will fire five rounds at target #1 (the circle in the upper left hand corner) on a count of "one-one-thousand, two-one-thousand," etc., up to "five-one-thousand." This will require a shot fired approximately every second.

Stage Two: Same exercise as above, into target #2 (the circle in the upper right hand corner) on a count of "one and two and three and four and five." This will require a shot fired approximately every half-second.

Stage Three: Same exercise as above, into target #3 (the square in the middle left) on a count of "1, 2, 3, 4, 5" as fast as the shooter can count. This will require all five shots to be fired in approximately one second.

Goal: The first string of fire allows the shooter to concentrate on trigger press and reset separately. The second string of fire will force the shooter to bring the two parts of the process together. The third string of fire forces the shooter to push herself to the limits of her ability. It's important to maintain the appropriate pace throughout the drill's strings, instead of relying on your perception of how long it should take to get defensively accurate hits.

Description: 5—7 Feet. If the shooter was able to keep all 15 shots on the targets, the distance can be increased 3—4 feet and repeated.

Things That a Coach Can Watch For: Watch for misses, especially on the slower paced rounds, which indicate that the shooter should return to the "SEB" or "Colored Numbers" drills.

Skill Level

INTERMEDIATE

Self-Led

Target: SEB Training Target

Skill Level

BEGINNER

Instructor-Led

Target: Official USPSA / IPSC Target

THE "SLAP, RACK, AND ROLL" DRILL

Description: Another favorite from Bill's Gun Shop & Range. The "Slap, Rack, and Roll" drill is designed to give the shooter opportunities to clear malfunctions while engaged in the exercise and to determine if he is prone to flinching in anticipation of the recoil. To conduct the exercise, an assistant will load the shooter's magazine with a mixture of live rounds and dummy rounds. When ready, the shooter will fire a full magazine.

Goal: This exercise allows the shooter to build appropriate neural pathways ("muscle memory") to quickly clear malfunctions. The shooter's goal should be to safely clear the dummy round while maintaining his eyes and muzzle on the target.

Distance: 21 Feet

Things That a Coach Can Watch For: Watch for the shooter to maintain his muzzle downrange when clearing the dummy round (which will require him to turn his body slightly, not the muzzle of the gun) and watch to see if he maintains his eyes on the target. Also watch for any flinch when the shooter pressed the trigger on the dummy round.

Alternatives:
» The assistant can also load the magazine into the firearm, which would allow him to have the top round be a dummy round.
» Place two or more dummy rounds in sequence.
» To simulate the effects of adrenaline on the hands, run this drill after holding your hands in icy water. In the northern states, an alternative is to leave your steel firearm in your car overnight on a freezing winter night, and shoot the next day on an outdoor range with no gloves. It's not fun.
» To simulate the effects of auditory exclusion, run this drill using the technique described in our "Auditory Exclusion" section in Chapter Five.
» An advanced version of this drill combines the dummy round exercise with either the "SEB" drill or the "Colored Number" drill.

FLASHLIGHT HOLDS

The flashlight holds described in this section offer a variety of methods for using a tactical flashlight to first illuminate a room or area to search for a threat, and then rapidly bring the muzzle in alignment with the light to engage the threat. All three holds have pros and cons, but it's fair to say that any handheld flashlight hold causes the fundamentals to suffer, and that these holds should be practiced frequently. Note that you can practice these holds on the range in full light to become comfortable with them, but we suggest that you invest in at least one session under true low light conditions.

FBI Hold

The FBI flashlight hold allows the light to be positioned in a variety of locations and momentarily flashed to check out your surroundings. Positions might include placing the light high and outside the body, above the head, or under the firearm. The theory with this hold is that if the light acts as a "bullet magnet," the changing light locations would confuse the bad guy about where you actually are. Drawbacks of this hold include the difficulty of lining up the light beam with exactly where you need to shoot. It also forces you to shoot one-handed, which is rarely as accurate as a two-handed hold (just ask Jack Weaver).

Harries

Like the FBI hold, the Harries still requires shooting one-handed, but the back-of-hand to back-of-hand pressure can steady your shooting hand. Ensure that you feel solid pressure between the backs of your hands, and are not simply resting the strong hand on the wrist of the support hand (picture holding a piece of paper firmly in place between your two backs-of-hands). Also, when setting up this hold ensure that you do NOT pass the muzzle of your firearm over your support hand.

Surefire/Rogers

Also described as a "cigar" hold, because it holds the flashlight between your index and middle finger. Best used with a light that has rubber rings around it to allow you to pull the flashlight tightly into your palm, which will activate a light with an end-cap activation switch. This hold keeps the light beam fairly aligned with the muzzle of the pistol, but with small motions of your palm, it allows you to move the light around. This flashlight grip comes the closest to allowing you to maintain all basic fundamentals, although it doesn't allow as solid a grip as you'd get with a mounted light and it still throws in the extra variable of activating the light, etc.

Skill Level

ADVANCED

Instructor-Led

Target: Official USPSA / IPSC Target

THE "LIGHTS OUT" DRILL

Description: The "Lights Out" drill is designed to give the shooter opportunities to gain experience with the different flashlight holds and/or a mounted light. We recommend that these drills be learned first in a full light environment before transitioning to a low light environment.

Goal: The goal of this drill is to safely gain experience with the different flashlight holds. There is no time limit specified which will allow the shooter to ensure she is performing each hold properly.

Distance: With two targets one yard apart at seven yards, start with the firearm and flashlight on the benchrest. On command, fire two rounds at each target. Shooter MUST NOT fire until the flashlight beam has lit-up the target. Repeat three times.

Stage #1, FBI Flashlight Hold—Lighted Conditions
Stage #2, Harries Flashlight Hold—Lighted Conditions
Stage #3, Surefire/Rogers Flashlight Hold—Lighted Conditions
Stage #4, Mounted Light—Lighted Conditions
(Note that firearm MUST be cleared prior to attaching mounted light)
Stages #5 to #8, Repeat the exercises above in low-light conditions. This portion of the exercise MUST be instructor-led until the student has proven proficiency in low light shooting situations.

Things That a Coach Can Watch For: Watch to ensure that the shooter doesn't cross her hand in front of the muzzle when setting up the Harries hold, and watch for her ability to place the light beam on target with all three flashlight holds. The FBI hold and Surefire/Rogers hold in particular can take time to master properly aligning the muzzle and beam of light.

Alternatives: An advanced version of this drill combines the "Lights Out" drill with the "SEB" drill, the "Colored Number" drill, or the "Slap, Rack, and Roll" drill. When performing the "Slap, Rack, and Roll" drill, ensure that the shooter has the flashlight's lanyard looped around her wrist so that the light can be "dropped" while performing the clearance procedure.

THE "LASER" DRILL

Description: The "Laser" drill is a scored exercise designed to allow the shooter to compare and contrast point/sight shooting to shooting with a laser.

Goal: The goal of this drill is to push the balance of speed and accuracy on all three stages. The "Comstock" scoring (which creates a composite score between time and accuracy) should give the shooter a good indication of how a laser might fit into his overall training and self–defense program.

Stage #1, Dry Firing

One target at seven yards, start with firearm on benchrest, dry fire five "rounds." Repeat three times. Focus on a solid grip and good trigger control. Instructor should watch for a "dancing" laser just prior to or after the trigger press. No score

Stage #2, Left Target, with Laser OFF, From the Holster

Two targets one yard apart at seven yards, start with firearm holstered, on command fire five rounds at LEFT target. Repeat three times. Scored Comstock (Score/Time)

Stage #3, Right Target, with Laser ON, From the Holster

Two targets one yard apart at seven yards, start with firearm holstered, on command fire five rounds at RIGHT target. Repeat three times. Scored Comstock (Score/Time)

Things That a Coach Can Watch For: On stage one, watch for the laser "dancing" just prior to or just after the trigger press, which can indicate a grip or trigger control problem. On stage three, watch for the shooter falling back on sighted fire. It may take several runs through stage three before the shooter learns to trust the laser and begins picking up his speed.

Alternatives: An advanced version of this drill combines the "Laser" drill with either the "SEB" drill or the "Colored Number" drill.

Skill Level

INTERMEDIATE

Instructor-Led

Target: Official USPSA / IPSC Target

WOMEN AND FIREARMS

We're tempted to pretend that there is an equal need for wives to get their husbands comfortable with firearms, but let's face it—firearms ownership has been a boy's club for more years than we can count. The great news though is that during the last decade there has been a dramatic shift in ownership and attitudes of women when it comes to guns. In part, that's due to firearm manufacturers recognizing that they were leaving out a major demographic in the products they developed and the marketing programs they ran, but in a larger sense, firearm attitudes have shifted among women at the same pace as other gender shifts in the job market and the military. Women are also realizing that they're very often their family's "first responder" when it comes to other emergency needs (from scraped knees to broken bones to the smoke detector going off in the middle of the night), and that attitude extends to what to do if the unimaginable occurs. Women also carry an unfair burden when it comes to violent crime. With more than 83 thousand rapes occurring in the U.S. in 2011, women are getting the fact that when seconds count and the police are minutes away, they'll need to depend upon themselves to end a violent attack *before* it's too late. For you guys, we have four recommendations if you'd like to assist your significant other in becoming more comfortable with the idea of using a firearm for personal and home protection:

» Buy your wife a copy of *The Cornered Cat* by Kathy Jackson. Kathy's book is written for women, and takes the approach that self-defense (and defense of family) is a personal responsibility that very often falls on the shoulders of the women of the house. Kathy's book also discusses shooting fundamentals, carry methods, and other topics strictly from a woman's perspective.

» Have your wife enroll in a women's only gun course, such as "Women on Target" sponsored by the NRA, or "Handgun Fundamentals, Ladies Only" at a Gander Mtn. Academy. While most guys who attend gun classes don't fit the stereotype that some people would have you believe, the "women only" approach guarantees that fact.

» Schedule time with your spouse at the local gun range, but schedule it for a non-peak time. Avoid choosing a lane next to shooters with large caliber guns, and be smart about what caliber guns you start *any* new shooter on. Nothing will take the joy out of shooting faster than starting new shooters (female *or* male) on a large caliber gun before they've worked their way up to it. One of our favorite training pistols is the .22 caliber Walther P22. It's small-framed, so smaller hands will have no problem getting a proper grip, and the recoil and "bang" are almost nonexistent. Besides that, they're great looking little guns (not that we're suggesting that women would choose a gun based upon looks alone). Most new shooters, even if they've bought into the negative stereotypes about guns, have a dramatic attitude change after their first trip to the range. They'll quickly realize that not only is shooting relatively easy, it's also *fun*.

» Keep the discussion on any gun-related topic to things that matter to you both, such as your joint responsibility to protect your children, and the fun you can have at the range. Just because *you* enjoy spending hours a day on gun forums debating the meaning of the Second Amendment, and fighting the "Glock versus 1911" war, doesn't mean that your spouse will like it. Come to think of it, if she finds out that you're spending hours a day on gun forums, she won't like *that* either.

» From biathlons to trap leagues, and from the USPSA to the Bianchi Cup, hundreds of options exist for women to become actively engaged in shooting sports. The NRA and other training organizations also offer specific classes set aside for women only, such as the NRA's "Women on Target" or Gander Mtn. Academy's "Handgun Fundamentals, Ladies Only."

"Freedom is never more than one generation away from extinction. We didn't pass it to our children in the bloodstream. It must be fought for, protected, and handed on for them to do the same, or one day we will spend our sunset years telling our children and our children's children what it was once like in the United States where men were free."

Ronald Reagan

RAISING KIDS AROUND GUNS

When it comes to kids and guns, you have two choices: Ignorance or education. But here's the reality—if you take the ignorance approach, your kids will get their firearms "education" from movies, video games, or from their friends. While we're not advocating that you take your four-year-old out shooting, we *are* advocating that you answer your children's questions about your firearms, and allow them to interact at a level that's safe for their age group. Regardless of how old your child is, you'll need to begin his or her education with an understanding of basic firearms safety. Here are a few safety tips that our family and extended family have used for kids of various age groups:

2—6 years old:

» Introduce your children to "Eddie Eagle" from the NRA, who teaches kids that if they see a firearm in an unsupervised situation, they should "STOP. DON'T TOUCH. LEAVE THE AREA. TELL AN ADULT." This isn't a "one and done" kind of education. Every single time you handle a firearm in front of your child, or any time the topic of firearms comes up, quiz them on this rule.

» As silly as it might sound, teaching your child to maintain "muzzle control" on his toy dart gun and to keep his finger out of the trigger guard until he's "on target" and is ready to shoot, will build that rule into his neural pathways, which will serve him for the rest of his life. At this age, a child's brain is twice as active as an adult's, and most of the brain's connections are being made. Anything they learn at this age stands a good chance of becoming hard-wired behavior.

7—12 years old:

» Depending upon your child's maturity and his or her ability to grasp all four Universal Safety Rules, as well as his or her *physical* ability to handle a firearm safely, this age group is ready to shoot a BB gun (or a .22 caliber rifle when they're at the upper end of this age group) under your close supervision. Make these sessions about abiding by the Universal Safety Rules and enjoyment, rather than treating it as a scored event. Personally, we'll ask our sons to recite the universal rules for us before we begin the "Shoot Small/Miss Small" drill (which is not scored) shown in this chapter.

» Regardless of how many times you have to say, "watch your muzzle" or, "take your finger out of the trigger guard," *keep* saying it. You own the responsibility for drilling these rules into your child's brain. They'll return the favor by doing the same with your grandkids.

» At the first hint of fatigue, or enjoyment turning into boredom, end the session for the day. Praise your child's accuracy, but even more so, praise them for the great job they did in adhering to the Universal Safety Rules, and review any time they failed to follow them.

13+ years old:

» Teenagers who have demonstrated maturity and rock solid safety when using a BB gun and .22 rifle, may be ready to step up to learning how to operate a handgun. With their shorter barrels, handguns can sometimes reintroduce muzzle control problems, so watch closely to ensure that all safety rules are being maintained.

So how will you know if your lessons are sinking in? In our house, we had a good indication on the success of our lessons when our youngest son (who was four at the time) told one of his friends, "Watch your muzzle!" as they were running around the house shooting their dart guns at everything in sight. Remember, as with all things in life, your children will learn more by watching what you *do*, rather than listening to what you *say*. Be a good teacher.

SO WHAT'S NEXT?

After finishing this book, we'll bet that your next question is, "So what's next?" We'll leave you with a few suggestions.

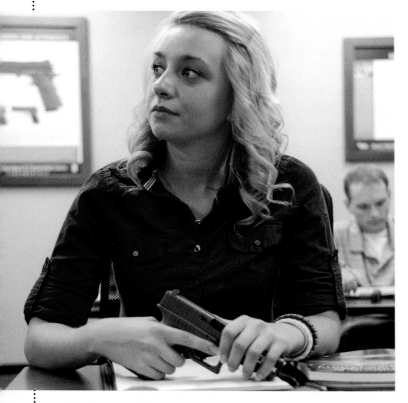

Take a Class

While many skills can be self-taught, the benefits of instructor led training for new shooters can't be understated. As mentioned in Chapter Three, practice makes *permanent*, so beginning your shooting experience with a skilled, experienced, and patient instructor can lead to a lifetime of enjoyment and success on and off the range, rather than a lifetime of bad habits. While many of the forty states that have adopted "shall issue" laws require some type of training before a permit is issued, those training courses typically invest a significant amount of time in discussing the laws of the state for which they're designed, rather than spending a large amount of time on basic firearm familiarization and safety. Our recommendation is that in addition to attending a "concealed carry" course in your home state, we suggest that you invest in at least one course that's *entirely* focused upon familiarization, shooting fundamentals, and safety. Our favorites include:

Gander Mtn. Academy. While not new to the firearms industry, the recently opened Academies offer a revolutionary program which includes education on basic handgun familiarization, concealed carry, and courses designed for women only. Gander Mtn. Academy not only provides a live fire range, they also provide virtual ranges and virtual simulators which push the student's speed and accuracy to the limits, all while placing the student in realistic life-or-death scenarios. For the closest Gander Mtn. Academy, visit **www.gandermountain.com/academy**.

Combat Focus Shooting. Owned and directed by Rob Pincus, Combat Focus Shooting is based upon the premise that the mind and body will undergo dramatic and immediate automated responses when under the extreme stress of a violent attack. In a CFS course, the range *is* the classroom, with a volume of fire doubling or tripling the volume of fire in competing courses. For a list of class dates and locations, visit **www.combatfocusshooting.com**.

>> While many skills can be self-taught, the benefits of instructor led training for new shooters can't be understated. As mentioned in Chapter Three, practice makes permanent, so beginning your shooting experience with a skilled, experienced, and patient instructor can lead to a lifetime of enjoyment and success on and off the range, rather than a lifetime of bad habits.

STOP

National Rifle Association. Locally, you're very likely to find dozens of NRA-certified instructors, capable of teaching everything from home defense to using a flintlock rifle. Our favorites include "Refuse to Be a Victim," "Basic Pistol," and "Personal Protection Outside the Home."

Join a League

While it might seem a bit premature for a new shooter to join a shooting league, we've found that national leagues such as the United States Practical Shooting Association are designed so well that new and expert shooters alike can enjoy themselves and continue to learn at the same time. Organizations like the USPSA not only dramatically increase shooters' speed, accuracy, and confidence, but they're also unflinching when it comes to safety, so participating in one of these leagues is a fantastic way to build those rules into our brains.

Join an Organization

While the Second Amendment has seen a great deal of forward progress in the last couple decades, that wouldn't have happened without the efforts of the millions of members of organizations such as the NRA, the National Shooting Sports Foundation, and the United States Concealed Carry Association. If you're not already a member, sign-up *today*. If you're a law enforcement officer who's looking for a new level of training, we can't recommend highly enough a decision to join the International Association of Law Enforcement Firearms Instructors (IALEFI). This organization is dedicated to making law enforcement firearms instructors more effective at training their students, and it succeeds wildly through the Master Instructor Development course.

Conclusion

We hope that you've found the information in this book useful, and we hope that you can put it to good use. Have fun at the range, shoot straight, and stay safe! In closing, remember that *you* are your family's first responder. Take that responsibility seriously, and use this right *wisely*.

Sniper Ed Kienzle of the Delaware County Pennsylvania Emergency Response Team, completes a combat shotgun drill while attending the IALEFI Master Instructor course in Cortland New York.

A RESPONSIBLY ARMED CITIZEN IS EDUCATED, TRAINED, EQUIPPED AND INSURED

WHAT YOU NEED TO KNOW IS...EVERY YEAR LAW ABIDING AMERICANS' PERSONAL AND PROFESSIONAL REPUTATIONS ARE DESTROYED BY CRIMINAL CHARGES AS A RESULT OF A JUSTIFIABLE USE OF THEIR FIREARM FOR SELF DEFENSE. IF YOU'RE FORCED TO USE YOUR GUN IN DEFENSE OF YOURSELF OR YOUR FAMILY, THE INSURANCE PROVIDED WITH EACH USCCA MEMBERSHIP WILL HELP YOU FIND, HIRE AND PAY FOR AN EXPERT PRO-2ND AMENDMENT LAWYER TO GIVE YOU THE BEST CHANCE IN THE COURT OF LAW.

USCCA MEMBERSHIP PROVIDES THE EDUCATION, TRAINING AND-MOST IMPORTANTLY— THE INSURANCE—TO ALLOW YOU TO CARRY YOUR GUN CONFIDENTLY WITHOUT HAVING TO FEAR LOSING EVERYTHING WHEN YOU'RE FORCED TO USE IT.

THE USCCA IS THE PATH TO BECOMING A RESPONSIBLY ARMED CITIZEN. JOIN TODAY. GETUSCCAMEMBERSHIP.COM

USCCA

NOTES

NOTES

NOTES

NOTES